BUDDIES: READING, WRITING, AND MATH LESSONS

Pia Hansen Powell

Routledge
Taylor & Francis Group
New York London

First published 2001 by Eye On Education

Published 2013 by Routledge
711 Third Avenue, New York, NY, 10017, USA
2 Park Square, Milton Park, Abingdon, Oxon OX14 4RN

Routledge is an imprint of the Taylor & Francis Group, an informa business

Library of Congress Cataloging-in-Publication Data

Powell, Pia Hansen, 1955-
Buddies: reading, writing, and math lessons / by Pia Hansen Powell.
P. cm.
ISBN 1930556-15-2
1. Peer-group tutoring of students. 2. Language arts (Elementary). 3. Mathematics—Study and teaching (Elementary)—Activity programs. 4. Education, Elementary—Activity programs. I. Title.

LB1031.5 P69 2001
372.139' 4—dc21

00-067722

ISBN: 978-1930556-15-7 (pbk)

Also Available from EYE ON EDUCATION

Teaching, Learning, and Assessment Together: The Reflective Classroom
by Arthur K. Ellis

A Collection of Performance Tasks & Rubrics: Primary School Mathematics
by Charlotte Danielson & Pia Hansen

A Collection of Performance Tasks & Rubrics: Upper Elementary School Mathematics
by Charlotte Danielson

Mathematics the Write Way: Activities for Every Elementary Classroom
by Marilyn Neil

Open-Ended Questions in Elementary Math: Assessment and Instruction
by Mary Kay Dyer and Christine Moynihan

Technology Tools for Young Learners
by Leni von Blanckensee

The Educator's Brief Guide to the Internet and the World Wide Web
by Eugene F. Provenzo Jr.

The Interdisciplinary Curriculum
by Arthur Ellis and Carol Stuen

Personalized Instruction: Changing Classroom Practice
by James Keefe and John Jenkins

The Paideia Classroom
by Terry Roberts with Laura Billings

Coaching & Mentoring First Year & Student Teachers
by India Podsen and Vicki Denmark

TABLE OF CONTENTS

PREFACE

I grew up in a family of six children. With 72 children on our block, we played games in our homes and yards, with whoever was available. We made exceptions and adapted our games for younger and older kids and knew who to ask for help when we needed it. We learned the rules and winning strategies with peer mentors and older coaches.

As a preschool teacher I worked with multiage groups of children. My public school teaching career began in a rural school with kindergarten through second-grade students. It seemed natural to work with individual students at their ability level and then to partner groups of children for independent practice. Building a sense of community among older and younger students was important for everyone's progress. Three years later, I found myself in a single-grade classroom looking for that "buddy" relationship with another class of students. We began with reading buddies, once a week. Students read books together. The conversations were rich with vocabulary and laughter. Big buddies cuddled their little friends in a rocking chair and focused their attention on the printed page. We knew these relationships were important for everyone.

Over the years, reading buddies became a popular schoolwide activity. When math standards and assessments impacted our world, raising math test scores was written in our school improvement plan. I approached one of the fourth-grade teachers in our building about collaborating once a week on a math standards lesson with our students. He agreed and we began. The activities we chose were based on our grade-level standards in mathematics and integrated literacy benchmarks. Our students couldn't wait for our buddy time. It was an academic and social success. The fourth graders becaame more comfortable with writing about math because of our teamwork.

This past year, as a Standards Specialist I worked with teachers on implementing our district standards in literacy and mathematics. I approached several teachers about "Buddies" and they were excited about the opportunity to work with other teachers and have their students benefit from the cross-age mentoring. We combined first graders with third or fourth graders, second graders with fourth graders, and third graders with fifth or sixth graders. We reorganized one group of second and sixth graders because we felt a four-year split was too great for the buddy work to be meaningful to both groups. We didn't want the big buddies to be just baby sitters. Students were held accountable for the time we spent together. The two classroom teachers and I would meet with approximately 50 students in the gym/cafeteria or a large classroom, once a week for an hour. This book is based on our model. It provides a guide for setting up a buddy program, sample lessons in mathematics and literacy, and assessment ideas that can monitor student progress.

About the Author

Pia Hansen Powell is currently an elementary school teacher and staff development facilitator in the Cheyenne, Wyoming public schools. Formerly a Standards Implementation Specialist, she was a Presidential Award winner for Excellence in Mathematics Teaching and is the co-author of *A Collection of Performance Tasks and Rubrics: Primary School Mathematics.*

1

Buddies: The Importance of Partnership for Children and Teachers

This book contains lessons that provide older and younger children in different grades opportunities to work together, one-to-one, on standards-based activities. These activities also enhance staff development for teachers in both content areas and in teaching practices.

The Benefits for Children

Young children benefit from having older students model appropriate social behavior and academic work. Country schools with multigrade classes and large families and neighborhoods used to socialize children this way. Times have changed, and many of our students no longer have the opportunity for interaction with cross-grade mentors. Schools can reinvent that spirit of community through regularly scheduled buddy work sessions with a variety of grade-level combinations. The sense of place, belonging, and purpose is crucial to the development of healthy children.

Classroom teachers have the ultimate responsibility for the planning, instruction, and assessment of current curriculum standards for a classroom full of students. Weekly buddy sessions provide the partner practice time needed for skills to take hold. Older buddies personalize the language, repeatedly demonstrate the lesson, and give immediate feedback to the younger buddy. For some students, this one-on-one time is the only extended time during the day when someone is listening and talking with just them! Teachers become guides that extend the lesson for more capable students and offer remediation for those few who might still need additional teaching points and time.

When older students mentor younger students, they gain the personal satisfaction of helping others. It inspires them to know that they can make an important contribution, a difference. Training our children to be good listeners, resolve problems, and make decisions has lifelong value. Honoring students who help others and affirming their positive impact on the academic success of younger students can encourage future community service. All students develop a capacity for learning together, creating, and communicating ideas. School becomes more like real life where people of all ages work together.

All students mentor, not just the brightest. Some of the most talented student mentors are those who don't learn in conventional ways. They enhance the learning in another manner. Their special skills are not always recognized in a single grade, traditional classroom arrangement. Physically large students, who are sometimes perceived as bullies, demonstrate genuine compassion in one-on-one relationships with younger buddies and become their allies on the playground. This creates a sense of fellowship within the school because children are engaged in meaningful relationships with other children.

Many teachers have combined classes of students for fun, interactive work. Although the experience is socially successful, it might have limited instructional value unless good planning, teaching, and assessment guide it. Buddy work is very much an adult-led activity. There are academic goals for each lesson and appropriate grade-level student expectations. Cultivating a positive emphasis on learning with student accountability is important to the program. The lessons relate to real-world situations, recognize various learning styles, and value multiple intelligences.

Some students prefer to work alone, and others learn best in groups. Although the lessons in this book are most appropriate for partner work, individual students may choose to work alone until they get comfortable interacting with a buddy.

THE BENEFITS FOR TEACHERS

Teaching can be an isolated profession. Teachers generally focus on their personal student population. Weekly buddy sessions encourage collaboration for planning lessons, providing immediate feedback, and assessing student understanding. Teachers' partnering also models cooperative group interaction for students.

Benefits for buddy teachers include time for self-analysis of teaching performance, renewal and recognition for professional success, an increased sense of efficacy, collegiality, and ultimately student achievement. Peer coaching and mentoring programs have provided this kind of support for individual classroom teachers in some school districts. However, these staff development models are not consistently maintained by many school administrations due to additional financial expenses. Buddy programs provide professional development at no additional cost to the school. New approaches are essential to cohesively align curriculum, instruction, and assessment practices with research on best practices in teaching and learning. Sharing responsibility for students, establishing the norm that all students can master challenging content, and generating a resource of effective teaching practices in the content areas are benefits of peer collaboration. Teachers who work together deliver a higher quality of instruction than teachers who work in isolation.

MEETING STUDENT NEEDS

Effective teachers are those who stimulate students to learn. Children learn best when they are absorbed in conversation and actively involved in hands-on experiences with a variety of manipulatives. Children need multiple opportunities and experiences in a wide variety of contexts to construct knowledge and understanding. During an inquiry, not all children are expected to notice the same things or reach the same levels of cognitive achievement. Individual team differences are respected and celebrated.

Language is a tool for learning and thinking. Reflection and metacognition, talking to others and thinking out loud, contribute to the process. Children who tell, draw, or act out a concept can teach another child and affirm their own understanding.

The greatest challenge in teaching is selecting the topics that will engage students in constructing their own learning and understanding. Allowing students to actively argue, inquire, and articulate their reflections takes time. When students really "know" something, they demonstrate the skill, communicate the concept, and perform the application in a new surrounding. Mentors for younger students need to know the content deeply, to teach it to their partners. Sometimes the younger buddy asks about something that actually clarifies the concept for the older buddy.

Questioning is a powerful tool for facilitating inquiry into topics of interest. It is important for teachers to model raising questions to clarify a lack of understanding and what the students want to know. Children will practice what they have heard their teacher do. Teachers take turns building an investigation, responding to the answers, and leading an activity that has depth and complexity. Deciding on an approach to solve a problem, getting the same answer in different ways, and expressing thinking processes are worthwhile group communications that foster this type of learning. Looking for patterns in the language and mathematics activities that will transfer to an advanced application of the concepts is the ultimate goal of these partnerships.

Brain research can be applied to buddy lessons as well. The learning environment for all students can be enriched when the educational content is challenging or new, and the students get interactive feedback. Problem solving, critical thinking, relevant projects, and complex activities provide this challenge. Problem solving can encourage the branching in the right and left hemispheres of the brain. Solving problems on paper; with a model, analogy, or metaphor; by discussions; with artwork; or with a demonstration exposes students to a variety of approaches to a task. The human brain reacts positively to the process, not necessarily to the correct solution. When the feedback is personal, specific, interactive, and immediate, all students benefit.

The buddy session begins with a mini-lesson, focused on keeping student's attention for approximately 10 to 15 minutes. The direct instruction is followed by process time with discussions, small group practice, and reflection. The lessons are summarized with brief journal writings that link the new learning to real-world application. Students are encouraged to share with other teams of buddies and compare their findings. The group work is often displayed on a bulletin board for future review.

GRADE COMBINATIONS AND CONSIDERATIONS

One size does not fit all! Generally, a two-year difference allows for all students to mentor at a competent level with compatible curriculum goals. Other combinations are certainly possible. Class size is a consideration. Primary classrooms generally have fewer students. Intermediate classes may have more students depending on yearly enrollment. Two older buddies may work as a team or older, responsible students can be asked to mentor two younger students. Partners sometimes work in groups of three. The idea is to focus on the capacity to serve students in a way that maximizes their learning.

There are 14 lessons for each of the major content areas: reading, writing, and mathematics. Within the lessons are suggestions for integration with science and social studies units. Due to the structure of the buddy relationship, reading, writing, listening, and speaking standards are part of every work period. There are also suggestions for lessons that are better suited in the beginning of the year. For instance, an interview lesson from the writing section would be more interesting to students just getting to know each other. The *My Buddy and I* book and the *Buddy Glyph* lessons build a sense of community and fellowship with the buddy teams. Teacher teams will ultimately make the planning decisions about which lessons to use based on their class experiences and grade-level expectations.

Although this book deals with issues applicable for elementary teachers, many secondary teachers have had great success with collaborative student work at multiple experience levels. First-year language students would benefit from oral conversations with third-year students who are writing conversations as part of an assignment on verb tense.

IMPLEMENTATION

The buddy spirit begins with the teachers! Teachers who share a common language about curriculum and teaching practices, choose to work together, and trust their professional relationship will be most successful.

PLANNING FOR BUDDIES

- Begin with a colleague who you enjoy working with. If you are new to a building staff, approach someone who seems interested in new ideas. If student achievement in mathematics is a school goal, perhaps several teams of teachers would work together on planning the lessons and sharing their ideas.
- Analyze the types and levels of support and resources available to you. Are there parents or educational assistants that could provide some additional supervision for individual student teams with special needs? What mathematical manipulatives are available in large quantities? Do you have enough copies of books you'd like to use? Clipboards are portable and work well if you are in a gym. Who will provide the pencils, crayons, scissors and glue required in some of the lessons?
- Identify factors like your school specialist schedules: art, music, P.E. recess, lunch, library, and computer times. Are there teachers who would like to get together but cannot find an hour in common? Is there a way to trade a specialist time with another teacher?
- Select a day and time, preferably once a week for an hour. Try to avoid scheduling field trips, guest speakers, and assemblies during the buddy time. The students really look forward to their time together. Is there an alternative time that would occasionally work?
- Identify a classroom area, gym, or cafeteria that would be available during the time you need. You'll need a general meeting area for the mini-lessons with a board for demonstrations, floor space for partner work and table space occasionally for writing.
- Provide your administration with the information related to your buddy plan: day, time, place, suggested activities, and assessments. Invite them to come and observe the students working together and share your academic plans. The noise level is sometimes high, but remember there are TWO classes, 50 students talking and doing active work. Let the office personnel know where you'll be.

- Solicit support from the special education teachers and preservice teachers. Because all students participate, some modifications are necessary and additional time is given to students to complete the projects. Another adult is invaluable, to process the activity, record student ideas, and provide encouragement to finish.
- Examine your time and energy. Communicate clearly about sharing the responsibility for planning and preparation. In theory, the more teachers that get involved, the less each single person should have to do. Make sure you're sharing the load. Alternate sessions with your colleague.
- Decide how you will evaluate student achievement, with rubrics or letter grades? Accountability is important for student performance. Will this be part of a language arts, mathematics, social studies, and science grades?
- Discuss how to improve and maintain the program for next year. Were the grade-level curriculum standards compatible? Was the time allotted and program site adequate for your needs? What lessons where the student favorites and yours?

TRAINING THE BUDDIES

The national standards movement has focused our elementary schools on raising student achievement. Yet, if you ask any teacher, coach, or youth leader, they would all agree it's the affective domain that must be addressed first. Due to the lack of structure in our current society, negative media influences, and the loss of direct supervision for our children, our schools are in desperate need of some plan that will address the character development of our students. Unfortunately, there is no time in the school day for an isolated curriculum, and the transfer of these practices from classroom learning to real-world application has been generally ineffective.

So, how do schools nurture respect, caring, responsibility and cooperation in students?

Teachers make character education an integrated part of each buddy lesson and classroom routine. Schools establish rules and regulations that are fair and reward good citizenship on a regular basis. Teachers model the cooperative social skills for students all day long. As a result of this environment, buddies have a more positive attitude toward their school, teachers, each other, and themselves because they are ultimately responsible for these interdependent relationships. Cooperative social behavior is modeled, learned, and analyzed by teachers and students regularly. Established routines and rituals take hold because they are daily habits.

Before the first buddy session, teachers may choose partners for their students based on personality and gender. Some teachers prefer to let the students find each other. Bright, capable younger buddies may need to be partnered with a more capable older buddy to keep them both challenged. A younger buddy that is developmentally delayed may benefit from a mature older buddy who can provide structure in a kind manner. Frequently, siblings will choose each other. There is no one perfect way. Within a group of 50 students, there will probably be one or two groups that need assistance because they are low functioning or exhibiting inappropriate, off-task behaviors. Usually the first buddy session is spent on "getting to know you" interviews. From that time on, students are encouraged to call each other by name.

Older buddies bear the greatest share of the responsibility for the quality of their work. They monitor the volume of their voices; they explain the concepts and encourage the younger buddy to participate. Teachers actively counsel how to express concern and give correction without negative putdowns. Older buddies encourage the younger buddies to share their rationale by paraphrasing their ideas. Positive mentoring interaction is infectious. When a student repeatedly chooses to make poor choices, he or she is asked to work alone on the group project or other schoolwork. Throughout the year, students resolve conflicts and communicate more effectively, but it's difficult to measure that kind of progress on a standardized test!

The younger buddies sometimes need to be encouraged to ask for help from the buddy, not the classroom teacher. Staying with the buddy, following directions, taking turns, and staying on task are the big issues for younger students. Focusing on one of these skills during each session usually works best. Brief discussions about how the activity felt and what the students struggled with gives teachers an idea about what area to work on next week. Each group is unique and will need to spend more or less time on specific social skills. Sometimes large spaces like a gym create an invitation for running wild. Reasonable and consistent behavior expectations need to be reinforced by all adults present. Consequences need to be predetermined by the teaching team.

Celebrations throughout the year, joint field trips, parties, and community service projects bond these students to one another. Opportunities to show their appreciation, acknowledge others, and switch buddies are important for both classes. When schoolwide buddy groups are established, the character curriculum is in place.

THE IMPORTANCE OF STANDARDS

Education standards express clear expectations for what our students should know at a classroom, district, state, and national level. Content standards relate to the essential knowledge and skills all children should master as set by our education organizations. Performance standards express the proficiency that students are expected to reach. The teaching and learning work in the buddy program reflect developmentally appropriate practices and educational standards. Every lesson specifically addresses instructional standards. These lessons may need to be adjusted to meet your local district interpretation of the standards. Activities are selected based on their ability to engage students in learning and understanding concepts. Assessments are embedded in the task, clearly expressed to students, and encourage accountability for the time students spent together.

The new standards are asking our older students to demonstrate proficiency on state exams in a format they have only recently been taught. For instance, the emphasis in mathematics has been on computation and getting the correct answer, using one method or formula. Now, our standards demand our students explain their thinking, show their problem-solving process and communicate their reasoning using models, numbers, and sentences. Students who are being tested in the fourth, fifth, and sixth grades have not all had the benefit of this type of instruction in the primary grades. We are testing challenging content in the context of an equally challenging assessment. Engaging these older buddies in this way of learning mathematics and literacy skills, with content that is comfortable for them already, allows them to practice the new assessment procedures without struggling with rigorous information.

Targets that define where we are going and why we need to get there are more likely to be achieved! Students eagerly embrace the concept of personal control over their score and often want to do more to "WOW!" the audience of teachers and other students. The confidence and positive attitude of both older and younger buddies is exemplary.

Buddy work can be an introductory activity, a practice time and/or a culminating activity. Students can be asked to teach a concept, play a game to reinforce a skill, or perform a final task to demonstrate proficiency. Teachers need to continually communicate with one another, to define the objectives of each weekly session. Objectives may vary according to individual students. Students may be at various levels of mastery and will therefore need differentiation. Most of these lessons are open-ended and are easily adapted to those special concerns.

Our educational contact time with students is limited and demands an integrated curriculum approach. Language arts lessons should reflect science and social studies units. Reading a weekly newspaper with a buddy and completing the charts, maps, and written work together is a simple adaptation appropriate for a buddy session. Active science discovery stations with buddies supervising and recording the data give everyone a one-on-one experience.

Mathematics lessons should require students to listen, speak, read, and write about their learning. This approach makes learning more meaningful for all ages of students and leads to student understanding. Involving students in intuitive ideas, active questioning, practice with ideas, and time to rethink hypotheses honors the investigating process. These "habits of mind" enhance all instructional areas.

ASSESSING FOR STUDENT UNDERSTANDING

Teacher observation remains a highly authentic assessment tool. Watching what children do and hearing what they say gives us important information about their learning. Two or more teachers cooperatively working with students provides an opportunity to question students on the application of the task, engage in conversation about concepts, and assist students with incorrect assumptions. Teachers can also share their interpretation of student work samples. This leads to rich conversations about student understanding and their capacity to apply knowledge and skills in new situations.

Open-ended prompts require students to think critically and prepare a response or product. In this case, there are multiple strategies for solving the same problem. Given time and verbal discussions, many students who traditionally don't excel in speed drills can contribute an analysis or synthesis of the task. Students are asked to construct a response to the problem and share with other buddy groups. Teachers can assess this work with rubrics and sample anchor papers. The expectations for student work are clear and consistent. For instance, in a math lesson about probability, the spelling of high-frequency words counts, along with legible handwriting.

Some buddy work can be extended to several work sessions. These types of assignments with partners are more like performance tasks and might require more complex investigations. For instance, a writing project that will eventually become a book will involve a prewriting, brainstorming session; the actual writing; the editing/review process; and the final publication. These projects may have to be done during individual class time *and* buddy sessions. Each work session should be assessed, as well as the final product. Visual models, oral discussions, and the completed communication all contribute to the total assessment score.

When looking at student work we need to ask:

- Can the student tell you what the task is?
- Do the students have an organized way to solve the problem or complete the task?
- Do the children see a relationship between this activity and the real world?
- Are the children able to self-correct when they make a mistakes?
- Can they see that there is more than one way to solve the problem and complete the task?
- Do they try different approaches? What happens when things don't work out?

Assessment is the process of gathering evidence. It needs to be based on multiple sources. The goals of quality assessments are to communicate with the student about their learning and impact future instruction. A four-point rubric provides students with specific guidelines for the lesson or project in the area of organization, accuracy, and presentation. When they complete the work required, they earn a score of 3. When they go beyond the standard, they earn a score of 4. If they don't complete the work or the journal reflection, they know they earn a 2. Even young students recognize the value of their work in comparison with a clearly marked target.

These rubric scores are used to communicate student progress in a consistent manner to the students, parents, and the community. The following rubric is a generic example of how teachers might evaluate the quality of student work. The actual finished product is often the final responsibility of the older buddy because of higher grade-level expectations. The buddy may want to finish writing the learning log at a later time, to work for a higher rubric score. The younger buddies can also receive partial credit for their contributions. Two scores may be appropriate for some activities. This book provides several rubric-scored examples of student work with commentary.

The results of each project are used to modify future lessons and provide individual coaching and enrichment. The focus of good assessment practices should reflect what is important for students to understand, and the application of the learning beyond the classroom. When assessment is relevant to the students, it is less of a chore and more of a celebration of the learning that is going on!

GENERIC RUBRIC

	4 Exceptional	3 Proficient	2 Developing	1 Novice
Organization of the Activity	All elements are clearly presented, shows complete understanding of the problem	Most of the elements are present, shows understanding of the problem	Omits a key element, shows an incomplete understanding of the problem	Omits several key elements, misunderstands the problem
Accuracy	Information is accurate and extended to another application	Information is accurate, project is completed	Information is mostly accurate, project is partially completed	Information is not accurate, project is not completed
Presentation/ Communication	Elegant, exemplary oral, written, and/ or visual presentation, Complete, sequenced oral, written and/ or visual presentation	Unclear and/ or incomplete oral, written and/or visual explanation	No explanation or solution	

2

Reading Activities

National reading standards for elementary grades focus on a variety of print materials including fiction, nonfiction, biography, and poetry genres. These texts should respect cultural differences. Students also need to read and interpret written directions, diagrams, maps, charts, graphs, and tables to apply their literacy skills across other curriculum areas. The expectation is that all students are proficient with these materials at their grade level.

- **Reading aloud** to students for 15 to 20 minutes a day in close proximity to the students increases literacy. Buddy reading time may look like this: The older student reads to the younger student. The younger student reads the same text back. The older student asks basic comprehension questions and records the younger student's answers on a graphic organizer. Best practices in teaching and learning support the importance of a reflection time in reading aloud. Just reading, without some personal thinking and partner communication, is not as effective. Shared reading with comfortable text embeds the language of the author in the students heads. Lessons should not be limited to just reading books but should include newspapers, magazines, and poetry. At-risk students gain fluency and comprehension with reader's theatre, choral reading, chants, and songs. Concepts about print and our grammar system are learned through this modeling. A child's curiosity, imagination, and visual memory are enhanced by read aloud activities.
- **Uninterrupted silent reading,** with text at an independent reading level, reading with a recorded tape, or following along with an older student, provides great practice for free choice reading. Beginning readers rarely read silently. They are dependent on the auditory feedback for assurance. Older buddies interview and complete reading response logs that identify the characters, setting, and plot in the story; describe the beginning, middle, and end of a story sequence; or engage in story rewrites.

- **Guided reading and literature group instruction** in small homogeneous groups is the obligation of the classroom teacher. It provides a consistent and systematic method of teaching students the skills and strategies they need to become proficient at their grade level. Teachers assess their student's reading levels and continually monitor the needs and strengths of each student.

Follow-up rereading with a buddy reinforces the skills learned in these mini-lessons. Older students can be taught to coach their younger buddy with the following prompts. When a child is stuck on a word, wait at least five seconds, then coach the student by providing the meaning of the word. Invite him or her to reread the sentence and read on. Look at the beginning sound and read on. As a last resort, tell the child the word. When the student makes a mistake that doesn't make sense, wait five seconds, then ask the student if it made sense. Invite the child to look closely at the word. Reread the sentence, put in the beginning sound, and if all else fails, tell him or her the word. Phonics is taught in the context of real reading, with a focus on making meaning. These strategies will help the older buddy, too.

Buddies can help younger students learn the names and sounds of the alphabet letters, word families, consonant blends, and high-frequency reading vocabulary words. The letters and words can be put on index cards, and students can play memory games, put them together in sentence form, and look for them in newspapers or the story books they are reading. Immediate feedback from a coach gives the younger student quality practice time. This is especially helpful in kindergarten through second-grade classrooms.

Buddy work can be woven into a family literacy program that encourages positive interaction between parents, caregivers, siblings, and students. Literacy programs provide training for parents regarding how to teach basic, age-appropriate, reading skills and can be expanded to buddy lessons. The more intensive, frequent, and long-term the support, the more successful the program will be.

BEGINNING, MIDDLE, AND END

STANDARDS ADDRESSED

- Reading comprehension and elements of good literature

MATERIALS NEEDED

- Reading book
- Record sheet for each team
- Pencils and crayons

DIRECTIONS TO THE STUDENTS

Opening: Today I will read a short story to you.

Let's see if we can summarize the parts of a good story.

What happened in the beginning? Share your thoughts with your buddy. How did the author get us involved in the story? What did you think would happen next?

What happened in the middle of the story? Share with another team of buddies. What problems came up for the main characters? What did you think would happen in the end?

How did the story end? What did the author do to make the story funny or sad, exciting or surprising? Share your ideas with a different team of buddies.

Now read your book with your buddy. When you have finished, complete the record sheet analysis of your story. What happened in the beginning, middle, and end of your story? Were there any surprises? Write your ideas in complete sentences.

Wrap up: Students who finish early can rewrite a new ending to their story on the back of their record sheet.

ASSESSMENT

When students write on their own, they need to be familiar with the structure of good stories. Reading and writing skills are highly integrated. Short children's stories lend themselves to an effective analysis that can then be applied to more complex books and personal writing. The record sheet provides an opportunity for students to demonstrate their understanding of story structure and reading comprehension. To score an advanced mark (4) on the task, students work must be thorough and synthesize the story structure beyond the obvious. This activity can be adapted for first- through sixth-grade work. The older students may need to be the record keepers. Remind them to write in print, not cursive, so the younger buddy can read the text, too.

BOOKWORMS

Name ______________________________ Date ______________

FOR BOOKWORMS

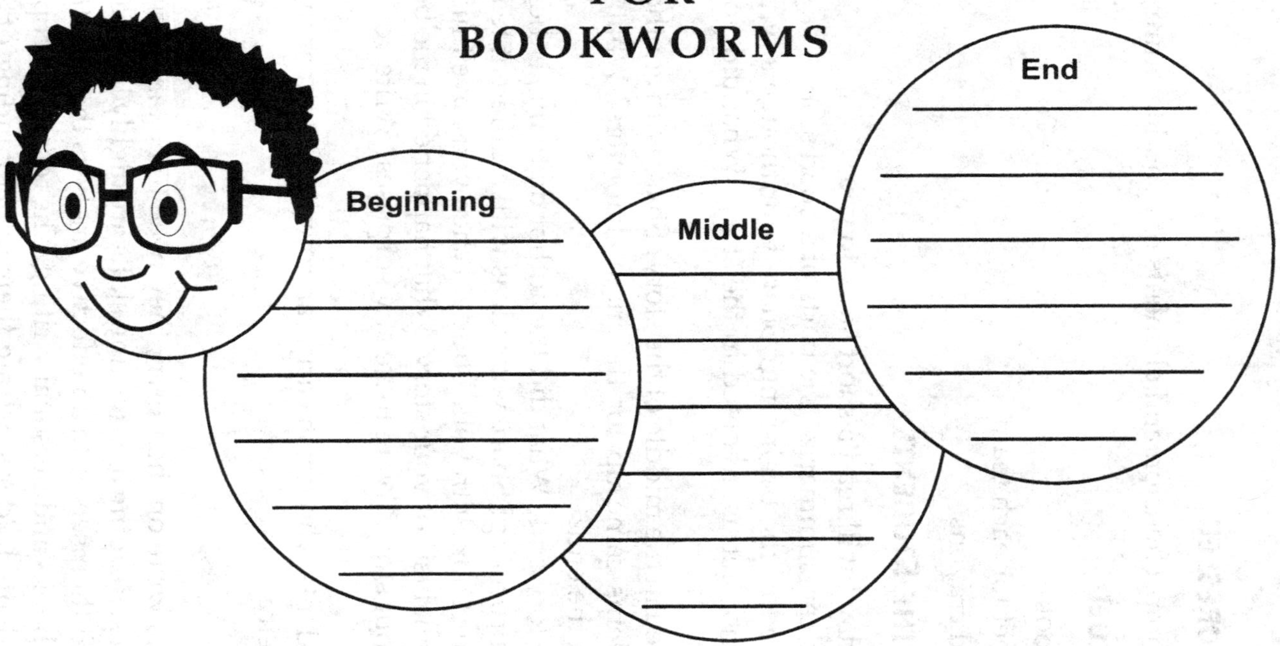

Title ____

Author ____

Score – 2. These students retold the parts of the story, but missed the true essence of the plot.

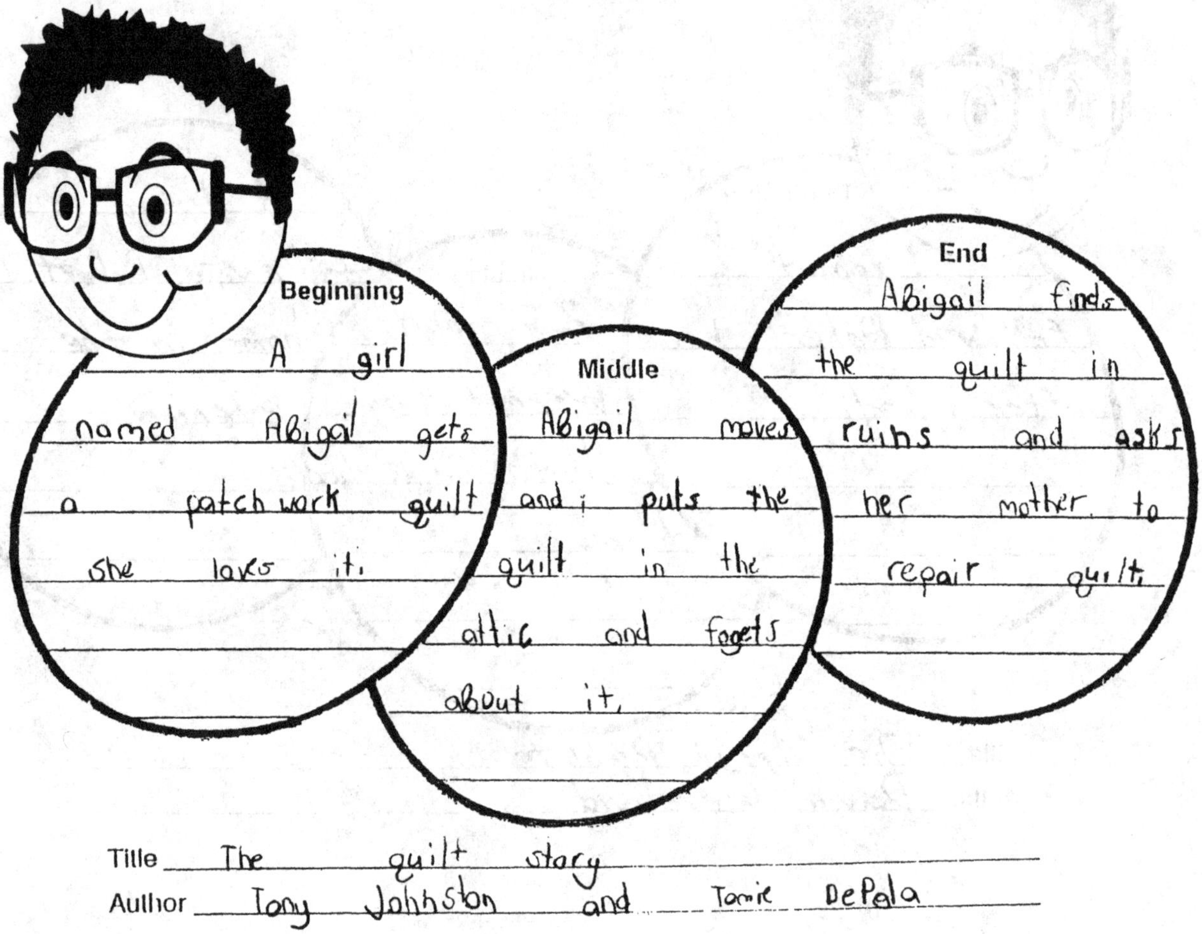

Score – 3. Elements of the story are represented accurately. Complete written sequence.

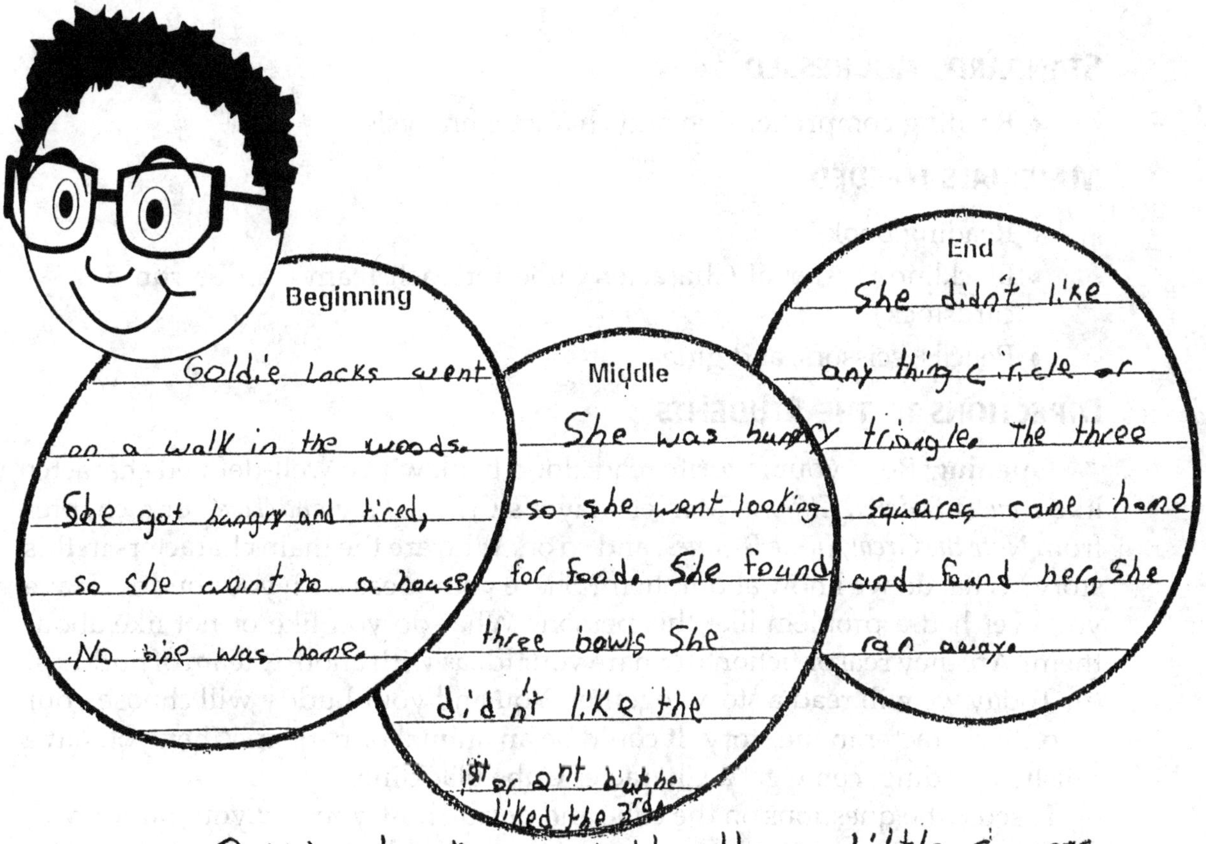

Title Goldie Locks and the three little squares.
Author Grace Maccarone

Score – 4. Students presented a complete understanding of the elements of good literature. Several written statements are sequenced and extended.

CHARACTER CUBE

STANDARDS ADDRESSED

- Reading comprehension and character analysis

MATERIALS NEEDED

- Reading book
- Blackline master of Character Cube for each team (can be run on cardstock)
- Pencils, scissors, and glue

DIRECTIONS TO THE STUDENTS

Opening: Read your favorite read aloud book with a well-defined character like *Amelia Bedelia, Clifford,* Mercer Mayer's *Critter, Frog and Toad,* or a chapter from *Nate the Great, Junie B. Jones,* and so on. Who are the main characters in this story? What do we know about them? Share your ideas with your buddy. Have you ever had a problem like this person? What do you like or not like about them? Are they real or fictional? Share your ideas with another team of buddies.

Today we will read a story together. You and your buddy will choose your favorite character in the story. It could be an animal or person. When you have finished reading, come get a Character Cube blackline.

Discuss the questions on the cube and decide how you and your buddy will answer them. Record your answers and complete all six faces of the cube. Cut the cube pattern out on the outside black lines and fold it in on the dotted lines. Glue it together.

Wrap up: Have students who finish early make a second character cube for another character in the same story, or share their cube work with other teams of buddies that have finished.

ASSESSMENT

The character cube is a fun way to analyze a character's strengths and weakness, sense of humor or adventure. To score an advanced mark (4) on the task, students would use complete sentences when appropriate and share insights beyond the obvious. This activity can be adapted for first- through sixth-grade work by choosing an appropriate book to read.

Students can use different stories or complete this activity with the same book and compare their observations with one another.

Additional activities that encourage students to analyze character development are to compare the main character to a person with whom they are familiar. These suggestions can replace a face on the cube.

CHARACTER CUBE PATTERN

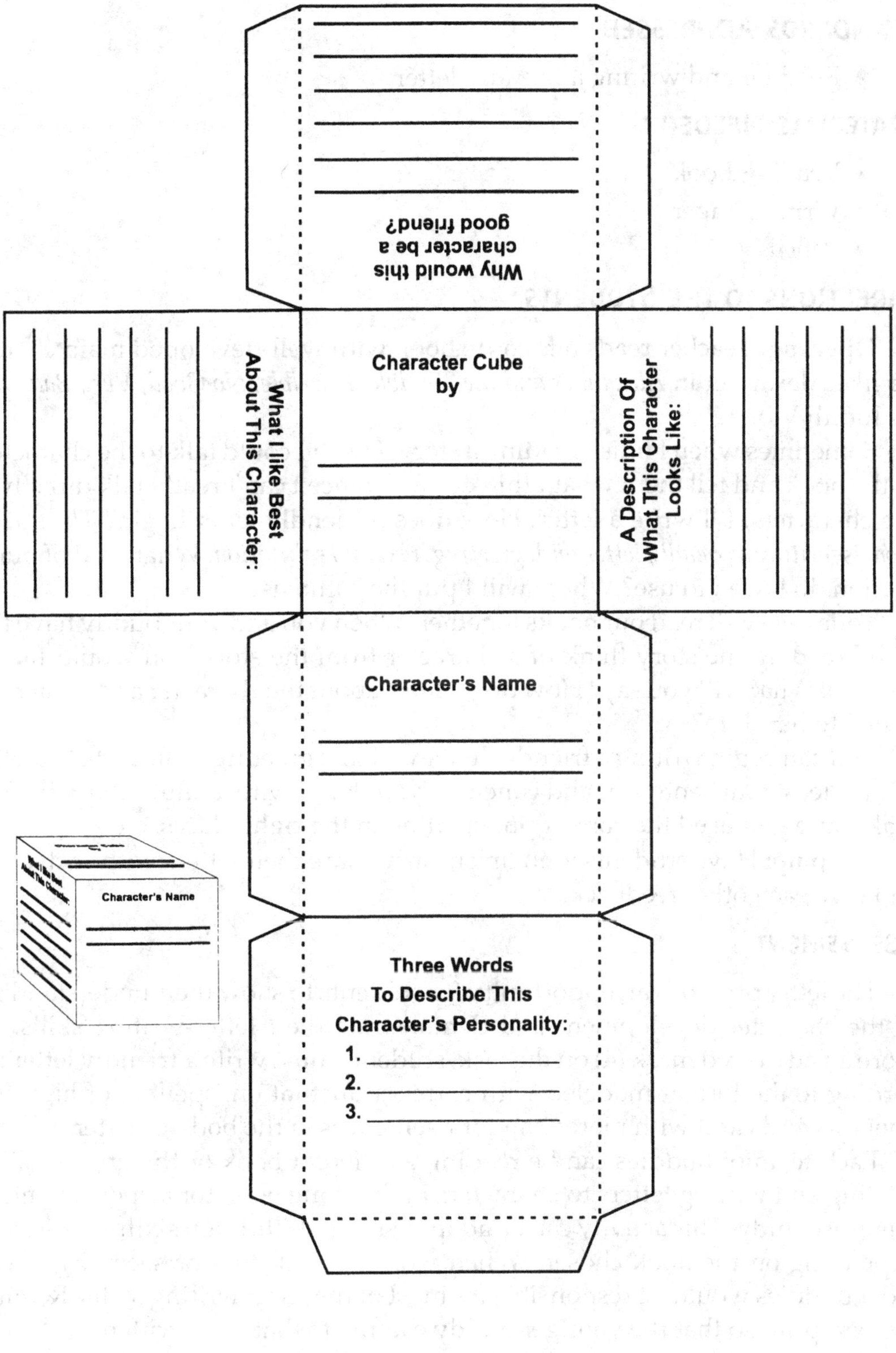

DEAR CHARACTER LETTER

STANDARDS ADDRESSED

- Reading and writing a friendly letter

MATERIALS NEEDED

- Reading Book
- Writing Paper
- Pencils

DIRECTIONS TO THE STUDENTS

Opening: Teacher reads a favorite book with well-developed main character like Alexander in *Alexander and the Terrible, Horrible, No Good, Very Bad Day,* by Judith Viorst.

Sometimes when I finish reading a story, I wish I could talk to the characters in the book and tell them what I think or feel. Since I can't really talk directly to the characters, I'll write a letter. How does a friendly letter begin? *The teacher models writing a friendly letter with greeting, text and salutation.* What kind of punctuation do I need to use? Where will I put the commas?

Today we will read our books together. When you and your buddy have finished reading the story think of a character from the story you would like to write to. What will you say? How do you feel about the character and what happened to her/him?

You can begin writing a friendly letter with the greeting. Complete the letter with at least four sentences and conclude your letter with a salutation. Check to make sure you used the correct punctuation in the right places.

Wrap up: Have students who finish early share their letters with each other and give each other feedback.

ASSESSMENT

The letter provides an opportunity for students to show their understanding of the character development and demonstrate their letter-writing skills. To score an advanced mark (4) on the task, students must write a friendly letter according to the format modeled with correct punctuation, spelling of high-frequency words and with more than four sentences in the body of letter.

Each team of buddies can be reading a different book or the group can be reading and writing letters to characters in the same book for a specific unit or literature study. This activity can be adapted for first- through sixth-grade work depending on the book chosen. When working with first or second graders, older buddies would be responsible for most of the letter writing skills. Remind them to print so that the younger buddy can read what was written.

Dear Hedgehog,

your friends wern't that much help.

Score – 1. *Hedgehog Bakes a Cake*. Incomplete. Students are missing several key elements, date, sentences, and closing.

Title is My mom and Dad make me laugh!

Dear Mom and Dad,

You make me laugh. Dad you wear stripes of all different sizes and shapes. Mom you wear polka-dots of all colors and sizes. Mom you like dots in the winter and summer too. Dad you like stipes on weekdays and weekends also. Mom and Dad you make me laugh!

Sincerely,
Your son

Score – 2. *My Mom and Dad Make Me Laugh*. Students restated the story but did not interact with the characters in this letter.

Dear Emery,

I feel sorry for you
because you didn'tnot
have any friends. I also
feel sorry for you because
you had to clean all the
dishes and and set all the
tables But I feel good for
you because you found a
good Friend.

Your friends
Pete Sam

Score – 3. *The 329th Friend.* All the elements are represented. Written presentation is accurate and organized.

Mouse Count

Dear Mr. Snake

I liked how you went and looked for the mice. Watch out Mr. Snake, mice can be very tricky. I liked how you cunted mice by mice. 1 mice, 2 mice, 3 mice, 4 mice 5 mice, 6 mice, 7 mice, 8 mice, 9 mice, 10 mice. I was wondering what kind of snake you were. We think you are a cobra by the looks of the picture. Sorry you didnt get to eat your ten mice for dinner. It was sort of funny when you thought that the big rock was a big mouse from your distance away from the rock. But when you went to look and try to get that big mouse it turned out to be a big rock. And when you came back to eat the other mice they had tipped over the jar and escaped and ran home. You shouldn't of left the other ten now you have no dinner to eat. You had a good book.

Sincerely,
Dan and Bill

Score – 4. *Mouse Count*. Exemplary written communication with all the elements clearly and accurately presented.

GIVE ME FIVE MAIN IDEAS

STANDARDS ADDRESSED

- Reading comprehension, elements of good literature, and main idea

MATERIALS NEEDED

- Reading book
- Record sheet for each team
- Pencils

DIRECTIONS TO THE STUDENTS

Opening: Today I will read this book (teacher's choice).

Let's identify the main ideas in this story. I will write your answers down on this chart paper (or white board) in complete sentences. *Who* was in this story? *What* happened to them? *When* did these things happen? *Where* did they happen? *Why* do you think they happened? These are the main ideas or elements of good literature that we'll analyze today.

Read your buddy book together. Complete the Give Me Five worksheet. Remember to use complete sentences to answer the questions.

Wrap up: Have students who finish early share their summary with other teams that have finished.

ASSESSMENT

A completed analysis of the elements of literature provides an opportunity for the students to demonstrate their ability to comprehend the main ideas. To score an advanced mark (4) on the task, students need to share insights beyond the obvious. This activity can be adapted for first- through sixth-grade work.

GIVE ME FIVE MAIN IDEAS

Names ____

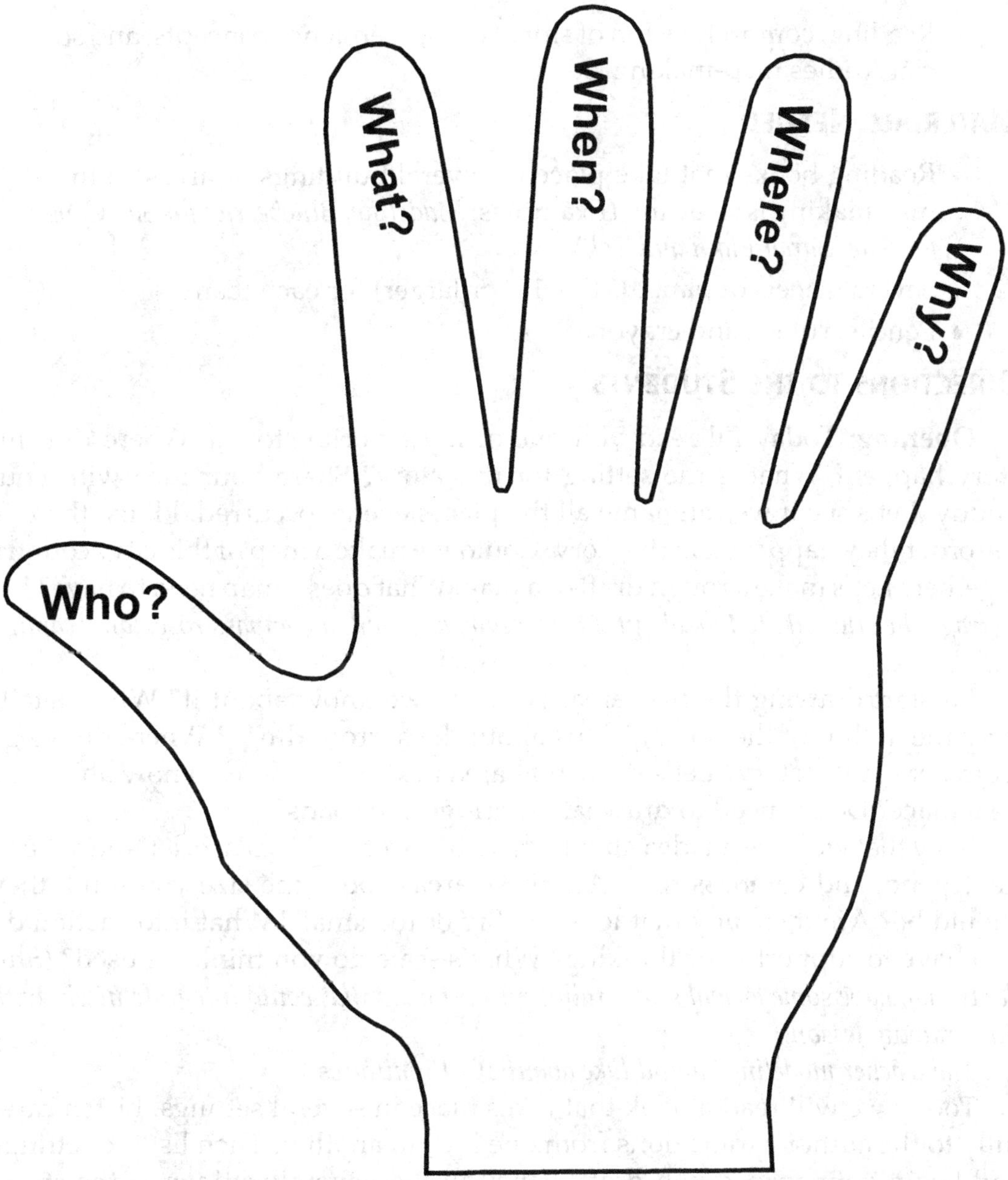

Title ____

MAPPING A STORY

STANDARDS ADDRESSED

- Reading, comprehension of story setting, sequence concepts, and social studies map-making skills

MATERIALS NEEDED

- Reading books that take place in several buildings or areas so that map making is relevant. (Examples: *Madeline, Blueberries for Sal, Caps for Sale, Sarah Plain and Tall*)
- Several sheets of paper (11" × 17" or larger) for each team
- Pencils, rulers, and crayons

DIRECTIONS TO THE STUDENTS

Opening: Today I'll read you one of my favorite stories. Where did this story happen? What is the setting for this story? Share your idea with your buddy. Let's see if we can name all the places events occurred. I'll list them in the order they happened in the story. Could we make a map of this city/country together? Let's make a rough draft of a map. What does a map need to have? *Encourage the students to talk about a title, scale, a legend, a compass rose, landscaping, and details.*

I'll start drawing the first area. What do we know about it? What details does the author of the book give us about the surroundings? Where do we go from here in the story? Let's draw that area next. What do we know about the next place? Do we need to draw lakes, bridges, or roads?

Now that we have an idea about where this story takes place, let's add the title, legend, and compass rose. Are these areas about the size you think they should be? Are there any that look too big or too small? What information do you have to support your thinking? What's scale do you think we used? *(Students may have some formal scale training in art class that could integrate nicely with this drawing lesson.)*

The teacher modeling should take about 10–15 minutes.

Today we will read a book that takes place in several settings. Listen carefully to the author's transitions from one area to another. Then list the settings and begin your map rough draft. Pencil in the general settings in the story. When you have a sketch you're comfortable with, get another larger paper and begin drawing your final copy. Make sure to use your rulers and pencils first. You can add crayon and lots of details later. When you are finished add your title, legend, and compass rose.

Wrap up: Have students who finish early reread their story to other teams and have the audience follow along with the map.

ASSESSMENT

The story map provides an opportunity for students to apply their understanding of the setting and story sequence concepts. To score an advanced (4) on the task, students must complete the project neatly, accurately, and with lots of details. This activity can be adapted for first- through sixth-grade work. Students can use different books, or study the same piece of literature and compare their interpretations.

This activity is important for students today because so many video screens are created for them in music, television, and movies. They don't often have an opportunity to imagine a scene themselves. This scene- and map-making process encourages them to listen for details in the story and visualize multiple settings in a sequence. It can be easily adapted and integrated with art and social studies standards.

MEMORY WITH WORDS

STANDARDS ADDRESSED

- Reading high-frequency words and partner practice

MATERIALS NEEDED

- Big book for teacher modeling
- Reading book for the younger buddy *at the instructional level*
- 3" × 5" index cards, about 30 for each team
- Pencils or markers

DIRECTIONS TO THE STUDENTS

Opening: Older buddies are coaches. Coaches can't run the race, but they can cheer their friend on! Today you will encourage the younger buddies to reread errors that don't make sense when they are reading. Wait five seconds after you hear the error. See if they can notice the error without your help. Then ask them if the word they used makes sense. Invite them to look at the picture and then reread the sentence. Let's practice with my book.

Teacher reads from a big book and models error making. Students pause five seconds and ask if the error makes sense. They invite the teacher to look at the picture and reread the sentence.

Whenever we read a new book, we have an opportunity to learn new reading words. As you read your book to your older buddy today, notice 15 words you'd like to practice reading again. When you have finished your book, write the name of the 15 words you chose, one word on each card. Have your buddy write the same word on a card, too, so that you'll have a pair for each of your words. Maybe it's a word that you stumbled on or a word with a new meaning. Make sure to print neatly and spell the words correctly.

When you are finished, you should have 30 cards. Now shuffle them and place them face down in a 5 by 6 grid (5 rows with 6 cards in each row). Now you're ready to play Memory.

The younger buddy starts. He picks up a card and says the word. Then he picks up a second card and says the word. If it is a match, he can keep the cards and take another turn. If they do not match, he returns the cards to their original location in the grid and the older buddy gets a turn.

The older buddy gets to flip two cards over and try to make a pair. If she gets a matching pair, she goes again. If not, it's the younger buddy's turn again.

The person with the most pairs at the end of the game wins. Make sure you read the word correctly, out loud each time.

Wrap up: Have students who finish early play another game. The younger buddy can take these cards home with the book to practice with family members.

ASSESSMENT

The assessment for this lesson is based on teacher observation of appropriate mentoring practices, with meaning errors in mind, recording 15 words twice correctly, and playing cooperatively. This activity can be adapted for third- through sixth-grade work by using more difficult reading material or science and social studies content area words.

NONFICTION READING TIMELINE

STANDARDS ADDRESSED

- Reading comprehension and story sequence

MATERIALS NEEDED

- Nonfiction book to read together
- Timeline record sheet for each team
- Pencils and crayons

DIRECTIONS TO THE STUDENTS

Opening: Read a piece from a nonfiction book during your read aloud time. Is this book true? Is the information accurate? Share your ideas with your buddy. What kind of book is this? *(Nonfiction)* How is it different from many of the other books we've read?

Authors of nonfiction books can present facts in many different formats. They can *report* on an animal, person, or event. *Procedural* nonfiction books are written to teach us how to do something. The author writes step-by-step directions, like a cookbook. In a *persuasive* format, an author tries to convince you to accept a point of view or position on an issue. A *narrative* book format allows the author to provide factual information through characters and settings more like a fiction story.

Reading nonfiction books helps us explore our world. We gain knowledge and understanding about things that we want to learn more about. Today when you share your book with your buddy, think about the author's writing style and all the facts in the story that provide valuable information.

When you have finished reading, complete a timeline record sheet. You will need to include all of the major events and a sequence of the procedures or a series of reasons that support a position. When you have finished the sequence analysis, write what you both learned from your book.

Wrap up: Have students who finish early share their observations with each other and give each other feedback.

ASSESSMENT

Students need multiple experiences with nonfiction genres to learn how to read for information, compare diagrams and charts, understand cause and effect, and draw their own conclusions. Nonfiction reading requires inquiry, a thinking process that challenges the reader to discover how these facts relate to the real world. A timeline is also an effective tool for a rough draft expository writing because it can organize and summarize the author's thoughts.

The record sheet provides an opportunity for students to share their understanding about nonfiction books. To score an advanced mark (4) on the task, students must complete the timeline sequence and evaluate the author's format with accurate insights. This activity can be adapted for first- through sixth-grade work depending on the selection of books.

NONFICTION TIMELINE

Title of Book ____________________

Names ____________________

We learned ____________________

____

PERSONAL DICTIONARY

STANDARDS ADDRESSED

- Reading decoding instruction with letter names, sounds, and vocabulary as a support for independent writing work

MATERIALS NEEDED

- A magazine, catalog, or old phonics workbook for each team
- A bound book with 27 pages (stapled or seamed)
- Pencils, scissors, and glue
- Published dictionaries available for student reference

This activity is recommended for the beginning of the school year so that it can be used by the students during their writing time.

DIRECTIONS TO THE STUDENTS

Opening: Read aloud an alphabet book like *Eating the Alphabet by Lois Ehlert* to introduce this activity. (There are many alphabet books that relate to thematic units of study that would also be excellent choices.)

Today we will make our younger buddies their own alphabet dictionary using pictures from these catalogs. Look for at least two pictures of something that begins with each letter in the alphabet. Cut out the picture and glue it down. Have the older buddy print the name of the word next to the picture. You will need to find at least two pictures for each letter of the alphabet. If you can't find a picture for a particular letter, you can draw something that begins with that letter. Don't forget to have your buddy print the word near your drawing. This dictionary will help your younger buddy when he or she writes stories and needs to spell naming words correctly.

Wrap up: Have students who finish read their dictionaries to each other.

ASSESSMENT

Quality pictures that name objects will provide an excellent writing reference tool. To score an advanced mark (4) on the task, students must have more than two pictures for most letters. Their dictionary should be neat and organized efficiently. This activity can be adapted for second- through sixth-grade work by making dictionaries with phonograms, homophones, and synonyms instead of single beginning sounds.

READ AND REWRITE

STANDARDS ADDRESSED

- Reading and analysis of story conflict and plot

MATERIALS NEEDED

- Reading book with an interesting conflict or plot
- Record sheet for rewrite plan for each team
- Writing paper for rewrite
- Pencils

DIRECTIONS TO THE STUDENTS

Opening: Read *If You Give a Mouse a Cookie* or one of your favorite stories with an interesting conflict or plot. Laura Joffe Numeroff wrote this book and then followed up with another book called *If You Give a Moose a Muffin.* Do you think we could rewrite this book with another character? What conflict would this character have? Discuss your ideas with your buddy. How would the plot develop? Share with another team of buddies. What ideas did you come up with?

Today each team of buddies will read their own book. As you share the story, consider what other character you could substitute in a rewrite and what his or her conflict might be if he or she played a major role in the development of the plot.

When you have finished reading, get started on a rough draft. Use the record sheet to draw and plan out your ideas. Make sure you have an interesting beginning, middle, and end to your story. You may use some of the patterns in the language of the original book, but construct your own conflicts. Make sure you're printing, not writing in cursive, so that your buddy can read the text. How will the conflicts be resolved? Will some conflicts be unresolved?

Wrap up: Have students who finish early begin writing their new story. This activity can certainly continue through a second session. Teams that finish first can start sharing their rewritten stories with one another. Younger buddies will remember the story plot even if they can't read all of it.

ASSESSMENT

The record sheet provides an opportunity for students to plan their story plot. To score an advanced mark (4) on the task, students will need to develop an engaging plot with multiple conflicts. The rough draft and final published work can be used as parts of the assessment. This activity can be adapted for first- through sixth-grade work depending on the story selected. Older buddies can select the book they will use from the school library, and each team can rewrite a different book. Or the teachers can choose the same book if it's connected to a science or social studies unit or literature read in class. The rewrites can then be extended to a compare and contrast lesson with an analysis of conflicts.

This lesson could be repeated several times during the year, as the students acquire advanced writing and reading skills.

READ AND REWRITE PREWRITING DRAFT

Names ______________________________

Title of Rewrite ______________________________

1.	2.
3.	4.

READ AND SPIN

STANDARDS ADDRESSED

- Reading comprehension and elements of a story

MATERIALS NEEDED

- Reading book
- Spinner blackline for each team
- Paper clip
- Pencil

DIRECTIONS TO THE STUDENTS

Opening: Read your one of your favorite books to the students. When I finish reading this story I will ask several people in our buddies group to retell parts of the story. Be ready! *(Have at least four students take turns using the spinner blackline. Each child spins the paper clip around the tip of a pencil. The teacher calls out what story component the clip landed on and the student explains the element to the group.)*

Depending on the sophistication of the buddy group, you can have the students evaluate the quality of the answer to determine if it was partially proficient, proficient, or advanced. Students will need to support their evaluation with specific information.

Today each team will read at least one book. When you are finished reading, take turns using the spinner to see who will retell different parts of the story. Each of you will spin three times.

Wrap up: Have students who finish early read another story together and use the spinner with the next book, too.

ASSESSMENT

Teachers observe students reading and retelling the elements of a story to demonstrate proficiency with reading comprehension. To score an advanced mark (4) on the task, students read more than one story and share an interesting analysis of the story elements. This activity can be adapted for first- through sixth-grade work with appropriate book selection.

READ AND SPIN: ELEMENTS OF A STORY

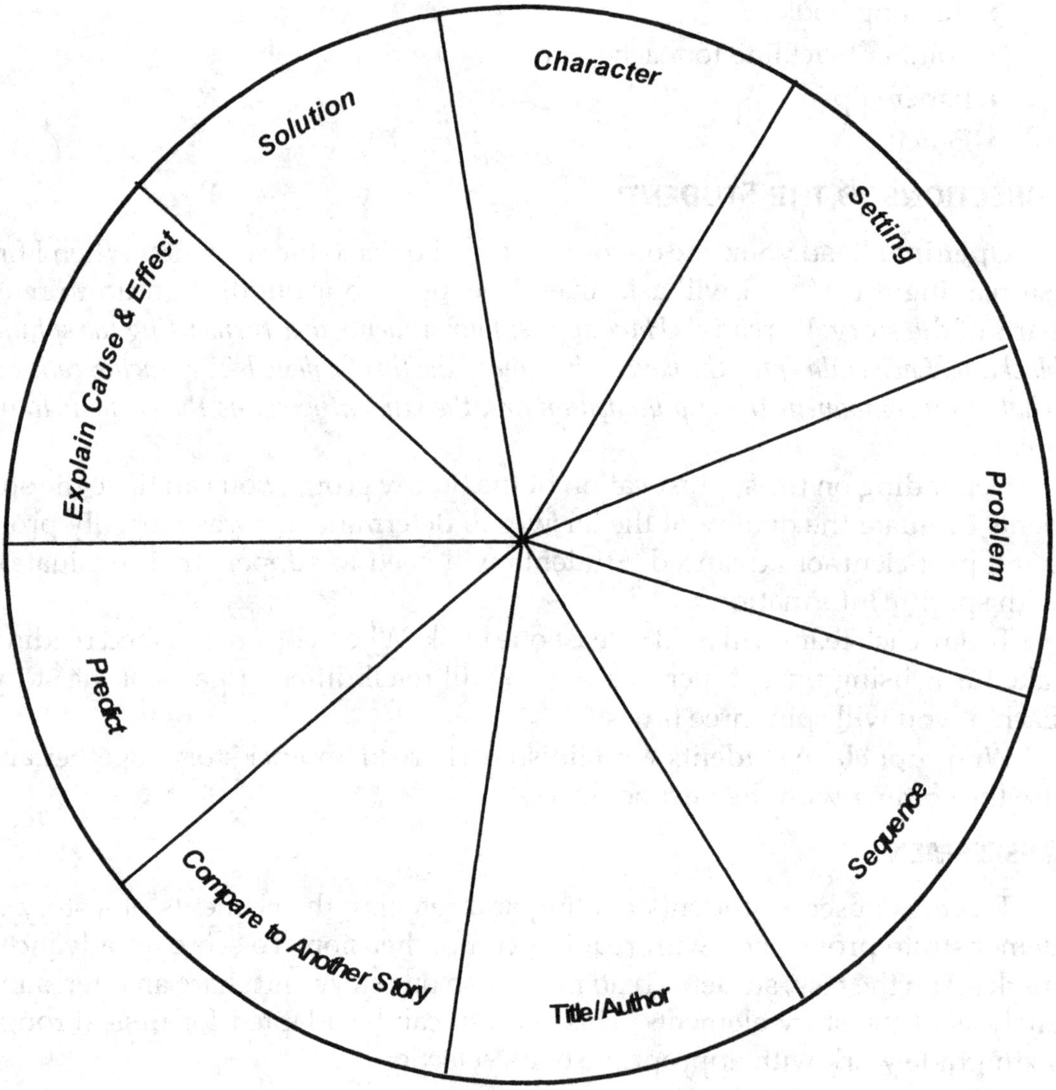

READING BOOKMARKS

STANDARDS ADDRESSED

- Reading and fluency during uninterrupted, sustained, silent reading
- Self-assessment of appropriate reading levels: independent, instructional, frustrating

MATERIALS NEEDED

- A difficult book and an easier book for the young buddy
- Bookmark blackline (can be run on cardstock)
- Stickers, stamps, templates, and stencils
- Markers and scissors

DIRECTIONS TO THE STUDENTS

Opening: I will try to read a really hard science book with lots of new words. *Teacher models struggling with difficult words.* If I could, I would like a scientist to read this book to me.

Now I'd like to read parts from *Rosie and Michael* with my partner teacher. This is a great book to read with a friend because there are two main characters and we can each read our part without too many problem words. *(Read this book with a partner teacher.)*

Sometimes I find a great book and can't wait to read it to someone else to see if he or she likes it as much as I did. I know the words and read it with expression. I want to see if my friend or family member laughs and cries at the same parts I did.

Read your first book with your buddy. After you finish, decide if this is a book that you could read all by yourself; was it easy for you? Was this a book you'd like to read with a friend or family member because you needed just a little bit of help reading some of the words? Was this a book you'd rather have read to you because it was frustrating? Too many new words!

Adult readers do the same thing. We pick books that are just right for recreational reading. We choose books for learning that we can get some help with. Sometimes we ask for help when the book is too hard.

We'll use the rest of our buddy time to create three different bookmarks for you to use with your favorite collection of books.

One bookmark will be for books you'd like someone else to read to you. The second bookmark will be for books you'd like to read with another person. The last bookmark will be for books you'd like to read to someone special. Be sure to put your name on each of your bookmarks.

When you have finished, see if you can find an example of all three kinds of books in the classroom or library collection.

Wrap up: Have students who finish early read their books.

ASSESSMENT

Students can use these bookmarks to identify books they find in the classroom or library they would like to save for buddy reading time. Encourage students to select a variety of books related to themes the class is studying, old favorites, and different genres.

When sending books home, parents are often concerned that their child isn't reading the book fluently. Sending a bookmark with a suggestion on how families can share the book is helpful.

Authentic assessment occurs when teachers observe students reading together and working cooperatively. To score an advanced mark (4) on the task, students must complete the bookmarks neatly, evaluate their reading abilities accurately and use their additional time for reading. This activity can be adapted for first- through sixth-grade work.

READING BOOKMARK BLACKLINE

Cut three bookmarks out along the black lines. Decorate them.

READING THE NEWSPAPER

STANDARDS ADDRESSED

- Shared reading and research

MATERIALS NEEDED

- A section of the newspaper (make sure the content is appropriate for children in elementary school)
- Record sheet for each team
- Pencils or highlighters

DIRECTIONS TO THE STUDENTS

Opening: There are many newspapers printed each day, all of which need to be edited for spelling, sentence structure, and content. Today we will research at least 10 examples of language patterns in the paper. You will highlight the word or sentence in the paper with a marker and write it down on your record sheet.

When you have finished the 10 required items, think of some other examples on your own. Remember to record the section, page number, and column where you located your work. Classify the item by what type of writing piece it was discovered in. Was it the news, a photograph caption, editorial, or advertisement?

Wrap up: Have students who finish early share their observations with each other and give each other feedback. Did they have any examples in common?

ASSESSMENT

The record sheet provides an opportunity for students to organize their research. To score an advanced mark (4) on the task, students must complete at least three additional quality examples. Their insights about the newspaper lesson are exemplary. This activity can be adapted for first- through sixth-grade work depending on the language patterns researched.

READING THE NEWSPAPER

Names____

Look in your newspaper and find at least one example of each of the following uses of our language. Record the section, page number, and column where you found it. Classify where you found it: news, photograph caption, editorial, or advertisement. When you have finished these 10, keep going. What else can you find?

Item	*Section*	*Page Number*	*Column*	*Classify*
A sentence with a ?				
A sentence with " "				
A noun				
A verb				
An adjective				
An adverb				
A preposition				
A pronoun				
A simile				
A homonym				

What did you learn today from the newspaper? ____________________

____

____

STORY BRIEF

STANDARDS ADDRESSED

- Reading comprehension and an analysis of character, setting, and plot

MATERIALS NEEDED

- Reading book
- Record sheet for each team
- Pencils

This activity follows many of the other suggested reading comprehension activities because it requires some previous experience with setting, characters and plot analysis.

DIRECTIONS TO THE STUDENTS

Opening: Before you read aloud a favorite book, read the brief description on the sleeve inside the front cover or on the back about the story. Then read the book.

When an author finishes writing a book, they often ask the editor or publisher to summarize the story in a brief narration. This narration must be short and to the point because it fits in such a small space. It helps people decide whether to buy or check out the book or leave it on the shelf.

Today we will read our books with our buddies and work together to write a brief description about the book. The narration should include critical information like the title, setting, characters, problems, important events, and the solution. To help you get organized, use the record sheet provided. Then write and edit your narrative piece.

Wrap up: Have students who finish early share their narratives with each other and give each other feedback.

ASSESSMENT

The record sheet provides an opportunity for students to organize all the elements of good literature for their narrative. To score an advanced mark (4) on the task, students must present their work accurately and with substantial detail. The final written narrative must be brief, complete, and interesting. This activity can be adapted for second- through sixth-grade work.

STORY BRIEF

Names ____________________

Title of Book ____________________

Setting:

Characters: ____________ ____________

____________ ____________

Problem:

Event 1: ____________________

Event 2: ____________________

Event 3: ____________________

Event 4: ____________________

Event 5: ____________________

Solution:

Title: A Three Hat Day

Setting: A Guy who likes Hats

Characters: R.R, baby, Ida, parents

Problem: R.R. was sad he's parents died

Event 1 R.R was alone in a big big house
Event 2 R.R. was very sad and wore 3 hats instead of two
Event 3 R.R. went to a huge huge hat stare.
Event 4 He grabed a hat out of the store and danced then a girl laughed at him and he cried.
Event 5 Then R.R. found a beutiful women.

Solution: R.R. had a baby with Ida and lived happily ever after

Score – 2. *A Three Hat Day*. Information is mostly accurate. The written presentation is unclear.

Title: Benny's Pennies

Setting: Town

Characters: Benny McBride, Sister, Mom, Dog, Brother, Cat, Mes. Hill, Michael Bess, Lucy May, Mr. Hopper, Mr. Beal

Problem: He had no more pennys

Event 1 Benny got a rose from Mes Hill

Event 2 Benny got a cookie from Lucy May

Event 3 Benny got a paper hat from Michael

Event 4 Benny got a ~~Bone~~ from Mr. Hopper

Event 5 Benny got a fish from ~~Mr. Beal~~

Solution: The family said thank you for all the stuff he gave them

Score – 3. *Benny's Pennies.* Elements of the story's character, setting, and plot are complete and accurate.

Title: Dinner at the panda palace

Setting: All the animals in town came to the Panda Palace.

Characters: panda 7.Hienas 3Pigs 10.chickens
1Elephant 8.penguins 4.Peacocks
2Lions 9.Bears 5monkeys,6.giraffes

Problem: There were so many animals in the palace, that there wasn't even room for a mouse.

Event 1 1.Elephant came in to the palace
Event 2 2.Lions came in to the palace
Event 3 3.Pigs came in to the palace
Event 4 4.Pecans came in to the palace
Event 5 5.came in to the palace

Solution: Mouse got a place to eat and it was the Elephants suitcase.

Score – 4. *Dinner at the Panda Palace*. Detailed analysis of the character, setting, and plot shows a complete understanding of the task.

WORD SEARCH

STANDARDS ADDRESSED

- Reading, high-frequency words, and vocabulary development

MATERIALS NEEDED

- Reading book
- Graph paper with ONE-INCH grid lines for each team
- Pencils

DIRECTIONS TO THE STUDENTS

Opening: Do you enjoy doing word searches? I do! Today when I read you a story, I would like you to remember at least one special word you think we should include in a word search about the book. *Teacher reads a favorite story.*

Share your idea for a favorite word with your buddy. Which words would you like me to use for a word search? I will list them on the board. *List at least 10 words. The teacher can use an overhead projector for this lesson or large chart paper.* I can write the words horizontally, vertically, diagonally, and backwards, too. Which direction should I write the first word? I am writing one letter in the each of the grid boxes.

I have written at least 10 words, so now I'm ready to use random letters to fill in the extra boxes on the graph paper, one letter in each box. The word search is complete when all the squares have a letter in them.

Now let's see who can find the first word. The word is _____. When you find it, circle the entire word with this marker. Where is it in the word search? Was it written vertically, horizontally, diagonally, or backwards? What does the word mean? Where did we hear it in the story? Who can use it in a sentence?

The second word is _______. Where is it in the word search?

Who can give me a definition for the word? Who can give me a synonym (homonym, antonym) for this word? Is this a word we heard more than once in the story?

3

WRITING ACTIVITIES

Primary students have so many stories to tell and no way to express their ideas in written form. Their fine-motor skills have not caught up with their ideas. Their spelling is based on limited consonant sounds they hear. They love to reread the things they imagined they wrote themselves, only to lose their place in the story. Older buddies can be excellent writing recorders. They know how to print, spell, and construct sentences that make sense. The older students have a reason to model their best penmanship! Sometimes they need to be reminded *not* to write in cursive for primary students. Then again, for students just learning cursive, it would be good practice to rewrite someone else's story.

There are several stages of writing. Kindergartners begin with pictures, scribbles, and random letters, and finally move into initial and final consonant sound writing. By the end of first grade, children master some vowel sounds and conventional spelling of high-frequency words. During their second-grade year, more students gain writing fluency. Modeled writing can be used to teach our language, conventions, content concepts, listening, reading, and composition. The young learner needs to have a scribe record their talking, refine the writing, and reread the thinking. The purpose of writing instruction is to make the children responsible for communicating their ideas and develop independence.

One-to-one conferencing allows the older buddy scribe to teach the writing skills as needed, encourage the younger buddy's approximations, and share the joy of writing about an experience. Writer's workshop is an excellent use of buddy time. Prewriting begins with brainstorming, webbing, drawing, and/or charting story sequences. The draft goes through a team, peer buddy group, and teacher edit review. It is revised with the intent to publish. Published work is then shared with the class or during a parent event at school.

Writing teachers have identified six important traits for good writing samples. Examine your school writing program and expectations. What do your students already know how to do? What should they practice? Older buddies should have already experienced direct instruction on the trait they are being asked to coach. The buddy mentoring sessions can focus on one of these traits at a time, or group several traits together for summative evaluations. Depending on the grade levels of the buddy groups, teachers may want to spend more or less time on each of the following structures.

- **Ideas and content** define the first trait of good writing. Pose questions like: Does it make sense? Do I know the subject well? Have I included interesting details? Do I have a purpose in this writing? Will it engage the audience to read the whole piece? Buddies can write for a short period of time and then compare their writing samples with another team of buddies. The discussion can focus on those questions. Students can get feedback and edit their work immediately.
- **Organization** is the second trait of good writing. Young children can string along many different ideas with lots of "ands." Their ability to think sequentially is critical to developing good writing skills. Primary students can work on creating three illustrations for a beginning, middle, and end to a story as a prewriting activity prior to meeting with a buddy. That way they are ready to tell an organized story when the buddy is available to write for them. The introduction should start out with a catchy idea. Everything in the story should tie together, building up to the good parts. It should be easy to follow and the ending should be interesting.
- **Voice** is unique to every student. It's what makes one student's piece easy to recognize from all the rest. The writing sounds just like he or she talks. The writer cares about the topic and expresses what he or she thinks. This is the most important hurdle to overcome with buddy teams. Many times the older buddies want to edit the younger buddies' voice so that it sounds like theirs. Big buddies can record the younger buddies' words and then rewrite the piece so that it reflects their personal voice. Teachers need to be sensitive to the writing conventions and semantic knowledge of the older students in relationship to the younger student's speech patterns.
- **Word choice** is another term for vocabulary enrichment. The best way to say something will come after a discussion where ideas are shared and respected. Words like *nice, good, fun,* and *very* permeate primary student writing. Older buddies can encourage a variety of vocabulary words, ask for clarification, and offer to substitute another word that would be a better descriptor. The goal is to have the reader picture it. Good writing should linger in the reader's mind.
- **Sentence fluency** and variety make a piece of writing interesting to read. Young children begin most of their sentences with high frequency word patterns like *I can, I like,* or *One day*. More experienced students know that sentences should begin in different ways. Some should be long and some short for emphasis. Writing should sound

natural. Buddies can take turns reading the text out loud and collaborate on the fluency of the sentences when they peer edit.

- **Conventions** have always been part of good writing practices. The intent of good writing is to share with others. Our language has certain conventions that need to be followed so that others can enjoy the work. Capital letters, ending marks, spelling, and paragraphing skills are developing in the elementary grades. Students can be each other's eyes when they are editing. This process saves the teacher so many petty corrections. Hopefully, by the time the teacher sees the buddy piece, it needs minimum revision for publication.

Writing with children is a delightful experience. When teachers partner with older mentor-students, they are not solely responsible for the help that younger students require. They have an opportunity to observe peer conversations, childlike humor, and individual student progress with the process. Older students may enjoy publishing these pieces of writing for younger buddies on the computer during their school day. That saves the primary teacher lots of time at the keyboard!

BUDDY COUPLETS

STANDARDS ADDRESSED

- Writing poetry, reading, listening, and speaking

MATERIALS NEEDED

- Paper for each student with an area for illustrations and lines for writing work
- Pencils and crayons
- Dictionaries available for reference

DIRECTIONS TO THE STUDENTS

Opening: Read a favorite rhyming poem from any collection by Robert Frost, Mother Goose, Lee Bennett Hopkins, or your favorite author. Most poets write in a variety of styles.

Today's lesson will be about writing poetry couplets. A couplet is a two-line poem that rhymes. Each line contains the same number of syllables.

Let's see if I can challenge you and your buddy to think of a second line to this couplet. If our topic of interest is space, I'll choose *The Earth* as my title. The first line of my couplet will go like this: *The Earth is round*. The last word in your couplet line will have to rhyme with *round.* Any ideas? Found, bound, hound, mound, pound, sound, wound.

How many syllables in that line? (See the Cinquain Poetry lesson for more instructional support with syllables.) Let's clap the syllables, The-earth-is-round-. It has four syllables. Can you create a rhyming line with four syllables with a rhyme at the end? Talk it over.

Let's hear your ideas. "I'm on the ground." "Water is found."

"Can't hear a sound." "Land is a mound." Which one do you like best? Great! Now let's recite the couplet together. How does it sound?

What other space-related topics could we write about? Stars, planets, moons, constellations, the sun, rockets, space stations, satellites, missions, or astronauts. We're ready.

Now you and your buddy are going to get started. The younger buddies will choose the first line. They will write it down on the paper. Then the older buddies will create the second line with the same number of syllables and a rhyme at the end. Put your heads together and brainstorm. You can use the dictionaries for help if you get stuck. When you're happy with your idea, write it down on the paper. Illustrate your ideas together.

Wrap up: Have students who finish early present their couplet poems to each other and give each other feedback.

ASSESSMENT

Poetry writing provides an opportunity for students to hear the rhythm, rhyme, and rich language that expresses our feelings in a poem. To score an advanced mark (4) on the task, the buddy poetry writing will reflect the students' understanding of syllables and rhyme. Exceptional word choice and a well-developed rhythmic pattern will be evidence of advanced work. This activity can be adapted for first- through sixth-grade work depending on the writing support provided for the younger buddy.

CINQUAIN POETRY

STANDARDS ADDRESSED

- Poetry writing, reading, listening, and speaking

MATERIALS NEEDED

- Record sheet for each team
- Pencils and crayons
- Dictionaries available for reference

DIRECTIONS TO THE STUDENTS

Opening: Read a favorite poem you love. There are many different forms of poetry. Can anyone name a type of poem? *Students may answer: rhyming, haiku, couplet, limerick, cinquain, chant, sonnet, alphabet, and shape poems.*

A cinquain poem does not rhyme. It has 22 syllables in only five lines. The pattern is two syllables, then four, six, eight syllables, and two syllables again. What is a syllable? Can you clap your name in syllables? Help your buddy clap his/her name. Stand up if you have only one syllable in your first name. Clap your name. Ready, set, go! Now let's have all the students with two syllables in their name stand up and clap their names. On the count of three: one, two, three. Does anyone have three or more syllables in their name? Stand up and we'll clap your name out. WOW!

Each line in a cinquain describes the topic, action, or feeling. The first line is usually the title, for instance, *Donut*. Donut has two syllables.

The second line will have four syllables, words that describe a donut. Any ideas? Share your thoughts with your buddy. What did you think of when I said donut? Cake, raised, glazed, powdered sugar, hole in the middle. What words could we use with a total of four syllables? Powdered sugar. Let's clap the syllables in powdered sugar. Yes, it has four syllables.

The third line will need six syllables and can describe an action. Share your ideas with your buddy. What action words did you think of? Eating a piece, tasting the sugar, sprinkling mess, dusting of white, dunking in hot chocolate or coffee. Great! We need six syllables. Will any of these ideas work? Which do we like best? "Dunking in hot coffee" has six syllables. Let's clap it. Yes!

So our cinquain poem looks like this so far:

Donut
Powdered sugar
Dunking in hot coffee

The fourth line has eight syllables and can describe a feeling we have about donuts. Talk with your buddy first. What ideas do you have? Soft, mushy, sweet, it's my favorite breakfast food, it's kind of fattening, but good to eat. Which of these words might work best? "My favorite breakfast food" has seven syllables. Can we add one other word to it to make eight? Let's try "sweet."

The last line has only two syllables. Are there any ideas we didn't use from the other brainstorming that you would like us to use with only two syllables? White dust. Good, let's try that.

Our completed cinquain poem would look like this:

Donut
Powdered Sugar
Dunking in hot coffee
My favorite sweet breakfast food
White dust

Teacher modeling should take about 10–15 minutes.

Today each team will use the record sheet to prepare for writing their own cinquain poem about any animal, food, or place. The record sheet will allow you to brainstorm and work out a draft copy before your final writing. Illustrate your finished copy.

Wrap up: Have students who finish early present their cinquain poem and give each other feedback.

ASSESSMENT

The cinquain poetry writing provides an opportunity for students to demonstrate their understanding of syllables, choose nouns, verbs, and adjectives that are specific to the topic, and present poetry to their peers. To score an advanced mark (4) on the task, the writing will reflect exceptional word choice and a well-developed final product. This activity can be adapted for first- through sixth-grade work. Students will be clapping the syllables out loud, so it may be a little noisy!

CINQUAIN POEM

Names ______________________________

1. Our topic has two syllables. ______________________________
2. Think of words that describe your topic. Record your ideas.

   ____

   ____

   Write the four-syllable combination of words you like best.

   ____

3. Think of words that describe an action related to your topic.

   ____

   ____

   Write the six-syllable combination of words you like best.

   ____

   ____

4. Think of words that describe a feeling related to your topic.

   ____

   ____

   Write the eight-syllable combination of words you like best.

   ____

   ____

5. Look back at some of your favorite words that you haven't used yet.

   ____

   ____

   Write the two-syllable combination you like best.

   ____

   ____

Copy your completed cinquain poem onto another piece of paper, illustrate it, and be ready to share.

1. Our topic has two syllables. Soccor

2. Think of words that describe your topic. Record your ideas.
I like to score
center forward

Write the four-syllable combination of words you like best.
I like to score

3. Think of words that describe an action related to your topic.
running, passing, shooting, Dribbling

Write the six-syllable combination of words you like best.
running, passin, shooting

4. Think of words that describe a feeling related to your topic.
hot, sweaty, thristy, happy, sad, fun, tough, easy

Write the eight-syllable combination of words you like best.
hot, sweaty, thristy, happy, fun

5. Look back at some of your favorite words that you haven't used yet.

Write the two-syllable combination you like best.
forwad

Soccor

I like to score
running, passing, shooting,
hot, sweaty, thristy, happy, fun
forward

Score – 3. Organization: Elements show an understanding of the task.
Score – 3. Accuracy: Complete and accurate syllable count.
Score – 3. Presentation: Not many additional words beyond the ones that were necessary.

1. Our topic has two syllables. Summer

2. Think of words that describe your topic. Record your ideas.
fun, hot, no school, sprinklers, sun, Lemonde stand,

Write the four-syllable combination of words you like best.
Lemonade Stand

3. Think of words that describe an action related to your topic.
swiming biking, baseball, rollerbladeing, skate boarding

Write the six-syllable combination of words you like best.
skate boarding fireworks

4. Think of words that describe a feeling related to your topic.
fun, hot, cold ice cream, barbaque

Write the eight-syllable combination of words you like best.
fun, cold ice cream, hot, barbaque

5. Look back at some of your favorite words that you haven't used yet. no school

Write the two-syllable combination you like best.
no school

Summer
Lemonade Stands
Skateboarding fireworks
Fun, cold ice cream, hot, barbaque
No School!

Score – 4. Organization: All elements of the task are clearly presented.
Score – 4. Accuracy: Brainstormed excellent options for syllables and word choice is extended. Poem is written accurately.
Score – 3. Presentation: Complete and sequenced written presentation.

COLOR MY WORLD

STANDARDS ADDRESSED

- Descriptive writing, reading, listening, and speaking

MATERIALS NEEDED

- Writing paper with lines for writing and an area for illustrations for each student
- Pencils and crayons

DIRECTIONS TO THE STUDENTS

Opening: Read *A Rainbow of My Own*, by Don Freeman, *Feelings*, by Aliki, or a favorite read-aloud book with a color theme.

Tell your buddy the name of your favorite color. Are there any buddy teams that have the same favorite color?

How do colors make you feel? Some people say that you are "blue" when you are sad. Yellow is a happy color. Do you agree?

Share your thoughts with your buddy.

Descriptive writing appeals to the reader's senses and creates a mood. We'll use color words today to express our feelings about some of our emotional experiences. Specific and personal details that intrigue our readers will engage them in the text.

We will each contribute at least one page to a class book about colors in our world and how they make us feel. Here are your choices:

- Was I ever "red" (embarrassed) when...
- I feel so "blue" (sad) when...
- You can color me "yellow" (happy) when...
- I'm so "green" (jealous) because...
- I was tickled "pink" (thrilled) when...
- I was "purple" with rage (anger) when...

Think about which of these prompts you'd like to complete. Each person will need to choose at least one. Older buddies will coach the younger buddies with spelling and handwriting concerns.

Illustrate your responses neatly. Check each other's punctuation and edit the final writing before you turn it in.

Wrap up: Have students who finish early write about another color of their choice. When several students are ready, share the writing and have the students give each other feedback on the quality of the writing and oral presentation. Choose a name for the class book. Have a few students illustrate a cover. Bind the buddy *Book of Colors* for future reading pleasure.

ASSESSMENT

This descriptive writing prompt provides an opportunity for students to demonstrate their proficiency with idea development, voice, word choice, and conventions. To score an advanced mark (4) on the task, the final product must be expressive and engaging with vivid words and phrases. This activity can be adapted for first- through sixth-grade work with vocabulary and writing support for the younger buddy. Remind the older buddies to print so that the younger buddy can read the completed work.

DEAR BUDDY LETTER

STANDARDS ADDRESSED

- Writing a letter, reading, listening, and speaking

MATERIALS NEEDED

- Chart paper or a board for teacher modeling
- Writing paper with lines for each student
- Pencils
- Dictionaries available for reference

DIRECTIONS TO THE STUDENTS

Opening: The other day I received a letter in the mail from a friend. I'd like to read it to you. (Read an actual letter or one you created.) Have you ever received a letter? Who was it from? What was it about? Share your experiences with your buddy.

Why do people write letters? Students' answers may include: They write letters to tell each other something, thank someone for doing something special, complain about something they are upset about, or ask for something they need or want.

What information is important to include in letter writing? Let's write a letter together to our principal. Letters usually begin with a date at the top so that we know when they were written. Let's write today's date including the month, day, and year.

Letters open with a greeting like *Dear*. Now let's spell the principal's name. We need to make sure to use capital letters for a proper name. The greeting ends with a comma.

Most letters have two or more paragraphs that explain the reasons for the correspondence. This is called the body of the letter. What should we say in our letter? We could tell him/her how our buddy time is going. We could share some of our favorite lessons. We might want to ask him/her to visit our next buddy session. What do you think? Share your ideas with your buddy. Who has a sentence in mind? How will each sentence begin? (with a capital letter). What will we say next? What other ideas tie together with our first sentence? Let's put those ideas together in a paragraph.

Each paragraph will be indented. All our statements will need to be complete sentences with capital letters and correct punctuation marks. Let's all reread our letter and see if there are any errors we need to edit.

A letter ends with a closing like *Sincerely, Your Friend,* or *Yours Truly* and then your name. How will we sign off on this letter? I'll make sure to deliver this letter to the principal today.

Teacher modeling should take about 15 minutes.

Today each of us will write a letter to our buddy with today's date, a greeting, at least two paragraphs for the body of the letter, and a closing. The letter can be written to thank the buddy, share a concern, or ask for something you need. Older buddies will be available to coach the younger buddies with spelling, punctuation, and editing comments. Older buddies may want to check in with their younger buddies for feedback on their letters, too.

Wrap up: Have students who finish early read their letters to one another and give each other feedback on the voice, sentence fluency, and organization of the letter.

ASSESSMENT

The letter writing process provides students the opportunity to demonstrate their understanding of voice, sentence fluency, and organization as traits of good writing. The buddy discussion and coaching promotes communication about the purpose of letter writing.

To score an advanced mark (4) on the task, the writing will reflect personal voice, varied sentences that link together in more than two paragraphs, and sequential organization. The letter will have grade-appropriate use of high-frequency words, spelling, and conventions. This activity can be adapted for second- through sixth-grade work depending on the writing support for the younger buddy.

Students can write replies to these letters, thank you letters to guest speakers and field trip hosts, letters to the editor of the newspaper about educational issues, and letters to request information from state or federal service agencies related to science and social studies units of study.

A letter to my buddy

Dear Jessica, You where a good buddy. Mathematics games where alway fun with you. You never cheated. You where alway good and sometimes I beat you in a game. And the best part was when we discovered that we had the same brithday December 28th wow your the most funest bestest one I Know. I hope you have a good Summer.

Score – 2. Organization: The visual model of a friendly letter is missing.
Score – 3. Accuracy: Date, greeting, body of the letter, and closing is complete and accurate.
Score – 4. Presentation: The written communication elegantly expresses the emotional relationship between these two buddies.

IF I COULD BE

STANDARDS ADDRESSED

- Persuasive writing, reading, listening, and speaking

MATERIALS NEEDED

- Writing paper with lines for writing and an area for illustrations for each student
- Pencils and crayons

DIRECTIONS TO THE STUDENTS

Opening: If I could be an animal, I would like to be a dog. I love dogs. They sleep in the house right by the owner's bed. They get to go on walks with their owner in good weather. They can play ball. They can go on car trips with the family and see the world. Dogs can play with other dogs and, sometimes, friendly cats.

If you could be an animal, what kind would you be and why?

Talk it over with your buddy. Can you agree to be one kind of animal? Discuss the possibilities and defend your reasons.

When you have decided on your team animal, begin your persuasive writing. You'll want to convince other people to agree with you, so be specific and try to influence their thinking. Remember to print, so the younger buddy can read the information.

Practice reading your piece of writing, so that your presentation is fluent. We'll share our work with other buddies.

Wrap up: Have students who finish early present their persuasive writing to one another and give each team feedback on the quality of their writing and presentation skills.

OTHER PROMPT IDEAS

- If I could be a body of water, I would be...
- If I could be a building, I would be...
- If I could be a song, I'd be...
- If I could be a food, I'd be...

ASSESSMENT

This persuasive writing provides an opportunity for students to develop their metacognition, prior knowledge, and inference skills with their buddies. To score an advanced mark (4) on the task, the writing will be convincing and influence other student's decisions. The piece will be organized and well supported with details and precise words to complete a picture in the reader's mind. The spelling and punctuation will be grade appropriate.

This activity can be adapted for first- through sixth-grade work depending on the writing support from the older buddies and the writing assessment criteria established for the primary students.

INTERVIEW

STANDARDS ADDRESSED

- Writing, research, reading, listening, and speaking

MATERIALS NEEDED

- Writing paper with lines for each student
- Pencils
- Dictionaries available for reference

DIRECTIONS TO THE STUDENTS

Opening: When I first came to this school as a teacher, I had an interview with the principal and several other teachers. They asked me questions about myself and about my educational background. These questions helped them to decide if they wanted to hire me. Interviews are very important in the real world, everyday. Employers have to plan ahead what questions they want to ask to get important information about the applicants. The applicants have to be well prepared with honest and thoughtful answers. Reporters plan interviews for radio, television, and newspaper work, too.

Think of a question you would like to ask your buddy. The question should elicit more than a yes or no response. The buddy should have to give you some information. Now ask the question of your buddy. Did that answer make you think of another question to ask? Now it's the other buddy's turn. Ask your question and listen to the answer from your buddy.

Let's share some of the good questions.

Now let's share some of the questions that didn't work as well. How could we make them better?

Teacher modeling should take about 10–15 minutes.

Today the older buddies will interview the younger buddies. The older buddies will think of at least 10 questions. They will write them down and record the younger buddies' answers.

Students need time to construct their own understanding of the quality of questions that will elicit the kinds of responses we've discussed as a whole group. Teachers can provide 10 or 20 questions as a format, but when the students pose their own questions, they're more invested in the learning process.

Examples of student questions:

- *What's your favorite color? Favorite sport?*
- *Do you have any brothers or sisters?*
- *When is your birthday? How old are you?*
- *What's your favorite soft drink? Favorite food?*

- *What's your favorite CD?*

Wrap up: Have students who finish early read their interview questions and information. The sharing will be more interesting if each buddy group has slightly different questions on their interview.

ASSESSMENT

This interview writing provides an opportunity for students to demonstrate their ability to research information through interview questions. To score an advanced mark (4) on the task, the interview will include more than 10 interesting questions and answers. The writing will reflect grade-appropriate use of high-frequency spelling words and punctuation.

This activity can be adapted for first- through sixth-grade work because the older buddies are conducting the interview. Remind them to print.

Younger buddies can conduct an interview with some additional writing support. The students prepare their questions prior to working with their partners. During the buddy session, they ask the questions, record the answers, and present their work.

Older buddies can take the interview information and write a descriptive paragraph about their buddy for a class book.

How old are you?
8
When were you born?
August 8, 1991
Whats your favorite color?
Green
Whats your favorite food?
carrots
Whats your favorite candy?
kit kat bar
Whats your favorite singer?
Christina Auguitera
Are you a male or female?
male
Do you have hair?
yes
Whats youn favorite NFL tean?
Broncos
Whats your favorite NBA team?
Lakers
Whats your favorite MLB team?
Giants
Whats your favorite NHL team?
Sharks

Score – 3. Organization: Asked 10 qualifying questions and recorded the information neatly.

Score – 3. Accuracy: Complete and accurate work.

Score – 2. Presentation: "Are you a male or female?" "Do you have hair?" were poor examples of interview questions.

What your favorite color? purple
What's your favorite sport? swimming
Do you have any brothers or sister? yes
How many brothers? two How many sisters? 1
When is your birthday? November 17 1990
What's your favorite soft drink? coke
What's your favorite CD? Christina Aguleria
What's your favorite state? Missouri
Who is your favorite BSB member? Nick
Whats your favorite brand of clothes? Brateny Speares
What's your favorite month? December
Who is your best friend? Jessica, Nikki
What do you like to do outside? jump on trapplians
What is your favorite subject? Art
Who is your favorite speciest? Mrs. Bloom

Score – 4. Organization: All 16 questions reflect a clear understanding of the process.

Score – 4. Accuracy: Questions were asked in a variety of ways. Students completed and extended the interview work.

Score – 4. Presentation: Written and oral presentation was exemplary.

MY BUDDY AND I BOOK

STANDARDS ADDRESSED

- Narrative writing, reading, listening, and speaking

MATERIALS NEEDED

- Each team will need at least 10 pages of paper that can be bound together later. Each page should have an area for illustrations and lines for writing.
- Pencils and crayons.

This is an excellent "Getting to know you" activity for the beginning of the school year.

DIRECTIONS TO THE STUDENTS

Opening: I am a _______ grade teacher. My hobbies are __________. My favorite foods are __________. I love it when ____________. I get mad when _________. What about you? Tell your story to your buddy.

Today we will write a short book about you and your buddy. Each of you will complete the first page with an "I am" sentence and draw an illustration that matches the text. Older buddies may coach the younger students with spelling or printing.

The next page will start with "My hobbies are." Each buddy will complete the sentence and draw an illustration.

The third page will start with a "My favorite foods are" prompt. Each buddy will write an idea and draw an illustration.

The fourth page will begin with an "I love it when" sentence. Remember to answer in a complete sentence and include the correct punctuation. What makes you happy? Draw a picture of what puts a smile on your face.

The fifth page will start with the sentence, "I get mad when."

What makes you angry, hurts your feelings, bugs you? Complete the sentence and illustrate your idea.

We only have an hour together, so you'll need to pace your time. Make sure you have all the written work completed before our class period is over. You may have some additional time later in class to finish the illustrations.

When you and your buddy have completed at least five pages, we'll collate them in a sequence, first your page, then his/hers. We'll bind the pages together to make a book about the two of you! Each of you will have a chance to take the book home to share with your families.

Wrap up: Have students who finish early add additional pages and put their books together. Their books can serve as models for the other teams.

ASSESSMENT

The book provides an opportunity for students to get to know each other through a narrative writing. To score an advanced mark (4) on the task, students must complete more than five narrative sentences with neat illustrations. This activity can be adapted for first- through sixth-grade work depending on the amount of writing support provided by the older buddy. Teachers can prepare the sentence prompts on each page so young children won't have so much to write.

Families will enjoy sharing the "buddy experience" with their child. When both buddies have taken the book home, keep the buddy books in the classroom for self-selected reading time. The books will be so popular they'll be read all the time, and the kids will learn special things about each other!

NAME POEM

STANDARDS ADDRESSED

- Writing, vocabulary enrichment, dictionary skills, reading, listening, and speaking

MATERIALS NEEDED

- Writing paper with lines for each student
- Pencils and crayons
- Dictionary, one for each team

DIRECTIONS TO THE STUDENTS

Opening: Teachers can read an example of a fun name poem from a collection by Shel Silverstein, Jack Prelutsky, Robert Frost, or any favorite author.

We'll begin with a friend's name: Jenny. Can you think of a word that begins with a "J" that might describe Jenny? Share your idea with your buddy. Who has a really good word to share with the group? Joyful, jealous, jumping, jubilant? Let's use "joyful" because Jenny is a happy person.

Can you think of a word the begins with the letter "E"? Talk it over with your buddy. Be ready to share your best idea. Energetic, excitable, envious, or excellent? Let's choose "energetic" because Jenny is so full of energy.

The next letter is "N." We need at least two good words for the letter "N" because there are two in Jenny's name. Brainstorm with your buddy. Let's hear your ideas. Nice, neat, nosey, natty, natural, night owl? Let's use the words "nice" and "night owl" because Jenny likes to stay up.

The last letter is a "Y." What ideas do you have for the end?

Talk it over with your buddy. Let's share. Youthful, young? Let's use the word "youthful."

Jenny's name poem will have five lines.

Joyful
Energetic
Nice
Night Owl
Youthful

Teacher modeling should take about 10–15 minutes.

Today each of us will make up a name poem with our buddy's help. Try to find some interesting new words in the dictionary that match the letters in your name. Read the definition of the word, and if it fits, use it to describe you. If you really get stuck, you may ask another buddy team for help.

Use your full first name, no initials or shortened nicknames.

Wrap up: Have students who finish early present their name poems to each other and give each other feedback.

ASSESSMENT

The poem writing provides an opportunity for students to demonstrate their understanding of new vocabulary words, use a dictionary as a reference manual, and present a finished product. To score an advanced mark (4) on the task, the writing will reflect exceptional word choice and a well-developed final poem. This activity can be adapted for first- through sixth-grade work by providing vocabulary and writing support for the younger buddy.

Joyful
Amazing
Couragous
Outgoing
Boywonder

Score – 3. Organization: The letters are represented.
Score – 2. Accuracy: Poem was mostly completed with the vocabulary enrichment and written support of the older buddy.
Score – 2. Presentation: Incomplete understanding of the vocabulary words.

Capable
helpful
risk taker
intelligent
skater

Score – 3. Organization: Shows an understanding of the writing project.
Score – 4. Accuracy: Word choice is accurate and extended beyond the obvious.
Score – 3. Presentation: Complete and illustrated with details.

Name Poem

Kind to people

Young and generous

Loving to animals

Excellent at soccor

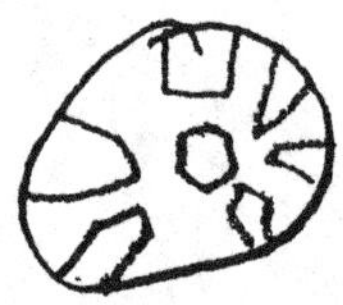

Score – 4. Organization: Elements are clearly represented.

Score – 4. Accuracy: Student had many extended ideas for each letter. Accurate and complete.

Score – 4. Presentation: Enthusiastic presentation; student suggested we do our last names next time!

POSTCARDS

STANDARDS ADDRESSED

- Writing, addressing mail, reading, listening, and speaking

MATERIALS NEEDED

- A variety of postcards from several places, used or new
- White construction paper cut in 6 x 9-inch rectangles
- Pencils and crayons

DIRECTIONS TO THE STUDENTS

Opening: Last summer I received several postcards from friends and family members who had gone on trips. (Show several examples of postcards) Have you ever received or sent a postcard? Share your answer with your buddy.

Why do you think they are called postcards? Why is the writing space so small? What happens when you're on a vacation?

Share your thoughts with your buddy.

Today we will write a postcard to our buddies. On the right-hand side of the postcard there are three or four lines for writing.

That's where we'll write our buddies' address. Ask your buddies to help you spell their first and last name, street address, the name of the city and state where they live, and their zip code. *(Primary teachers may need to provide this information for younger students who may not know. A written example of a mailing address may be provided on the board or chart paper.)*

How will we begin our card? Dear — or Greetings from —?

Now write at least three sentences that express your enthusiasm or humor about this trip. It can be something that really happened on a trip you took or something that you think could happen. How will you end your card? Your friend, Miss you, See you soon?

You can make up your own postage stamp for the top right corner. How much does it cost to mail a postcard?

When you have finished the written side, you are ready to design your own postcard picture. Think of someplace you have been or would like to go. Draw a detailed illustration of that special place.

Wrap up: Have students who finish early share their postcards with each other. Completed postcards can be "mailed" to each buddy's cubby or desk.

ASSESSMENT

The postcard writing provides an opportunity for students to practice their own personal address, addressing mail to others, and writing brief detailed text. To score an advanced mark (4) on the task, the writing will include more than three sentences, with an accurate mailing address and neat illustration. This activity can be adapted for first- through sixth-grade work by providing additional writing support for the younger buddy. Encourage older buddies to print their text so the younger buddies can read it.

RECIPE FOR A BUDDY

STANDARDS ADDRESSED

- Writing, reading, listening, and speaking

MATERIALS NEEDED

- Writing paper with lines for each student
- Pencils
- Sample cooking recipes for student review

DIRECTIONS TO THE STUDENTS

Opening: If I wanted to make chocolate chip cookies, what ingredients would I need? Share your thinking with your buddy. Let's make a list of all your ideas. Sugar, chocolate chips, flour, salt, eggs, butter, brown sugar, baking soda, sometimes nuts or oatmeal. This list will really help me when I go to the store and get the ingredients, but how will I know how much sugar to get? Or how many eggs? What other information do I need?

Recipes for cooking and baking give us directions. They tell us how much of what ingredients to put into the recipe, in what order, and how long it will need to be cooked or baked. Writing accurate and detailed recipes is very important because if you forget something or put too much of an ingredient in, your food won't taste very good.

When you use a recipe, it is really important that you read the directions carefully and follow each step carefully.

Each team will write a recipe for being a good buddy. Think about what ingredients would make a good buddy. What qualities are important to you? List your ingredients first.

How much of each characteristic would you like in your perfect buddy recipe? Record the amount in teaspoons, tablespoons, and cups. You can use fractions, too.

Then tell us how long your recipe will have to cook or bake. How many minutes at what temperature? You are welcome to look at other recipes for ideas, but make sure yours is original!

Wrap up: Have students who finish early share their Good Buddy Recipes with each other.

ASSESSMENT

The recipe writing provides an opportunity for students to think about the characteristics of being a good buddy. The buddy dialogue about patience, humor, responsibility, and manners is an important relationship building exercise. To score an advanced mark (4) on the task, the writing will include insightful word choice, accurate use of quantity expressions, and sequential directions for a final product. This activity can be adapted for first- through sixth-grade work depending on the writing support provided for the younger buddy. Remind the older buddy to print the text so that the younger buddy can read it.

REVISING AND EDITING

STANDARDS ADDRESSED

Writing, reading, listening, and speaking

MATERIALS NEEDED

- A draft writing piece for each buddy
- Pencils
- Dictionaries available for reference

DIRECTIONS TO THE STUDENTS

Opening: *(Read a brief piece of your personal draft writing.)* Most of the time when I write a story, my first attempt is not my best. I need to ask myself some editing questions like: Do I have a beginning, middle, and end in the story? Are the sentences and paragraphs in the right order? Did I follow punctuation rules? Are all the words spelled correctly? Did I use descriptive words and phrases? When I read my writing a second time, I can think of suggestions that will make the piece better.

Editors are writing coaches who help authors improve their skills. They use certain symbols to mark the corrections they suggest. The author can then make the changes and revise the final copy.

First, our older buddies will be our editing coaches. They will listen while we read our story. They will discuss the following questions with us about the rough draft.

- Is the story interesting and original?
- Is the message organized clearly?
- Did the reader feel a connection with the writer?
- Are the words chosen with a purpose?
- Does the story read smoothly, and are the sentences varied?

The coaches will make some verbal suggestions to the younger buddy writers. These are recommendations. Think about the reasons behind the ideas. Do they make sense? Will the writing piece still sound like the younger buddy wrote it?

Then the older buddies will reread the story for writing conventions. These are the editing marks they will use:

- Capitalize the letter
- Make a lowercase letter
- Missing punctuation
- Add something
- Take something out
- Look up the spelling
- Indent a new paragraph

When you have discussed the editing comments, the younger buddies will rewrite their pieces. The final draft will be the younger buddies' responsibility. Older buddies will be evaluated on the use of correct editing marks and the quality of their suggestions on the draft copy.

Older buddies may work on their own writing pieces next. Ask your younger buddy to listen to your story and give you feedback on the structure and organization of the writing. Edit your own work for punctuation and spelling errors. You may ask another older buddy for help with conventions. Rewrite your piece.

Wrap up: Have students who finish early present their final copy to one another and give each other feedback.

ASSESSMENT

The writing process improves student vocabulary development and use of the dictionary as a reference tool. The six-traits inventory evaluates the quality of the organization, voice, and sentence structure in the writing piece. To score an advanced mark (4) on the task, the writing will be clear, organized, and compelling. This activity can be adapted for second- through sixth-grade work. First graders usually edit their short writing pieces with their teacher.

Older buddies should have some prior experiences with editing written work. However, it is easier to practice editing skills on shorter pieces of writing. Remind the older buddies to be positive, but honest, with the younger buddies. Specific suggestions directed at the writing will be most helpful.

If there are some struggling older buddy writers, have one of the teachers join their group and supervise the editing process. It will be a worthwhile lesson for all the students.

STORY STRIP

STANDARDS ADDRESSED

- Writing, reading, listening, and speaking

MATERIALS NEEDED

- Comic Strips from the newspaper, two or three for each team
- Record sheet for each team; may be enlarged to an 11×17-inch paper to give younger buddies more room to write
- Pencils and crayons
- Dictionaries available for reference

DIRECTIONS TO THE STUDENTS

Opening: Read your favorite comic strip. Newspapers have a section in the paper with comics. How many of you have read the comic or funnies section of the paper? Comic strips tell a story. They have to be well organized and sequenced to make sense. Cartoonists use talking and thinking bubbles to communicate their message. Thinking bubbles looks like this. Talking bubbles look like this. (Model the thinking and talking bubbles format on the board). The illustrations in each frame need to have lots of details because people count on the pictures to understand the humor or irony in the story.

Each buddy team will look over several comic strips from the newspaper. Read the text in the talking or thinking bubbles together and pay close attention to the illustrations. What do you notice about the way the cartoonist developed the story?

Now you and your buddy will create your own. Brainstorm some possible ideas. Who will your characters be? People, animals, make-believe characters? What will happen in your story? Something funny, sad, or adventurous? Think of a beginning, middle, and end to your story. Where will your story take place? Inside, outside, in the city or country, in this galaxy or another? How will the problems be resolved? Will it have a happy ending or a funny one? Talk it over and choose your best ideas.

Work together on the Story Strip Record Sheet. There are eight frames all together. Make sure to finish your story by the last frame. Use talking and/or thinking bubbles to communicate your ideas. You may use the dictionary to look up the spelling of the words you're not sure of. Print neatly and put lots of detail in your drawings. Color your pictures if you have time.

Wrap up: Have students who finish early present their story strip to each other and give each other feedback on the organization and sequence of the story.

ASSESSMENT

The comic strip style of writing provides an opportunity for students to demonstrate their understanding of organization and story sequence. To score an advanced mark (4) on the task, the writing will have a clear sense of beginning, middle, and end. The main ideas will be supported with precise illustrations.

This activity can be adapted for late first- through sixth-grade work depending on the writing support for the younger buddy. Remind students to write the words first and then frame the words in a bubble.

STORY STRIP RECORD SHEET

Names ____

Story Strip Title ____________________________________

WANT ADS

STANDARDS ADDRESSED

- Writing, reading, listening, speaking, and social studies

MATERIALS NEEDED

- Want ads from the newspaper, several for each team
- Large group graph with two columns and tape
- Writing paper with or without lines for each team
- Pencils
- Dictionaries available for reference

DIRECTIONS TO THE STUDENTS

Opening: Teacher reads several want ads for services and goods. The classified section of the newspaper has several kinds of paid advertisements for lawn care, painting, and baby sitting services, and lots of used cars, furniture, bikes, etc. The paper sells the advertisement space by the line or sometimes by the word. The customers try to be thrifty and keep their text to about 25 words. When the newspaper office receives all these advertisements, they put them in categories. The editor will put all the employment advertisements together. The car ads will be separated from the apartment advertisements, and so on.

Today, we will sort these classified ads in two groups: goods and services. I have a two-column graph ready for us to use.

Services are things that people can do for each other. What kind of advertisement would offer a service? Share your idea with your buddy. Now let's share as a group. Give me your best ideas. *Nurses* provide what type of service? What do *teachers* do for others? What kind of service do *secretaries* provide? How about *carpenters, plumbers,* and *welders*?

Goods are things that people can make, buy or trade. What kind of ads do you think you might find for goods? Share your idea with your buddy. Now share with the group. Things that people sell in a garage sale or flea market are goods. People sometimes buy things they don't need or want and then sell them later, like furniture, toys, and clothes. Things we buy in department stores, retail stores, and groceries are all goods.

Today each buddy team will look over several classified ads from the newspaper. Read the words carefully and decide with your buddy if this ad is about buying and selling goods or providing a service. Cut the advertisement out, write both your initials in the corner, and put the ad in the correct graph column under GOODS or SERVICES. Be ready to defend your position.

Teacher checks for students' understanding as teams graph their ads. Mini-lesson should take approximately 15 minutes.

Now your team is ready to write your own ads. Think about what good you both would like to sell. You can only use 25 words to describe this thing in such a way that people will want to buy it. What information will you need to include? Descriptive words with the color, price, size, condition, or age of the item might be helpful. Be specific, accurate, and concise. Print neatly.

The second classified advertisement will be for a service you both could provide. What chore do you know how to do really well? What are you really good at? Share an idea with your buddy. Reading books to someone, tutoring other people with math problems, delivering a newspaper, cleaning a room, picking up trash, washing dishes, making cookies, mowing the lawn. What information will you need to include in the text so that people will want to hire you and pay you for your service? Your ages, experiences, references, enthusiasm, and previous training would be important. Choose each word carefully because the ad cannot be more than 25 words. Be explicit and accurate.

Wrap up: Have students who finish early present their classified ads to each other and facilitate discussions about goods and services.

ASSESSMENT

Classified advertisement writing provides an opportunity for students to practice descriptive writing with precise vocabulary. The social studies concept of goods and services is reinforced through real-world examples. To score an advanced mark (4) on the task, the writing will have a clear, well-supported message with exemplary word choice.

This activity can be adapted for second- through sixth-grade work. Advertisements can also be sorted into needs and wants categories. Food, clothing, and shelter are all needs; toys and recreational pursuits are considered wants. This is a valuable lesson for our students today!

WHO AM I?

STANDARDS ADDRESSED

- Narrative writing, reading, listening, and speaking

MATERIALS NEEDED

- Record sheet for each person
- Pencils

DIRECTIONS TO THE STUDENTS

Opening: I will tell you about someone in this room. Listen carefully to the details, and see if you can guess whom I am talking about.

This person loves sports, likes to read, appreciates a good movie, and if he/she were a teacher, he/she would teach art. Who can that be? How can we find out? Ask your buddy if it could be him or her. Does this describe anyone's buddy?

What made it easy to figure out? What information would have made it more difficult? What information would have made it easier?

When writers want to tell a story, recount a personal experience, or report on an event, they might choose to write a narration.

Today we will write a narrative about our buddy using specific sentence starters. The buddy needs to answer the sentences honestly. We will share these writings later with each other and try to figure out whom the narrative is about.

Ask your buddies to finish the sentence and record their answer on their record sheet. When you have completed the narrative, you may add additional sentences on the back.

Wrap up: Have students who finish early practice reading the narratives to one another. When you have a small group of finished writings, play detective and see if the students can guess whom the narrative is written about.

ASSESSMENT

The record sheet provides an opportunity for students to organize their autobiographical narrative writing. To score an advanced mark (4) on the task, students can extend the writing beyond the suggested information. The writing should be well organized, with accurate high-frequency word spelling and punctuation. This activity can be adapted for first- through sixth-grade work depending on the written work required of the younger buddy.

WHO AM I?

1. I love ______________________________

____

2. I like ______________________________

____

3. I believe ______________________________

____

4. Someone I'd like to get to know better is ______________________________

______________ because ______________________________

____

5. I have accomplished ______________________________

____

6. I would like to ______________________________

____

7. I appreciate ______________________________

____

8. If I were a teacher I would ______________________________

____

Who Am I?

1. I love my family

2. I like football

3. I believe in myself

4. Someone I'd like to get to know better is Michel Jordan because he is my favriot b-ball player

5. I have accomplished Elemantry school

6. I would like to grow up ~~at~~ doing drugs

7. I appreciate adults

8. If I were a teacher I would try and give the kids a good education.

Score – 2. Organization: Elements are limited.
Score – 2. Accuracy: Student needed prompting to complete task.
Score – 2. Presentation: No depth in communication about why.

Who Am I?

1. I love my dog because he is funny and nice.

2. I like soccor because you run alot.

3. I believe in good luck

4. Someone I'd like to get to know better is John Mabley because he never gives up.

5. I have accomplished 2nd place in art fair

6. I would like to play sting when I get older.

7. I appreciate Harry Potter books.

8. If I were a teacher I would give no homework! But add an extra hour to school!

Score – 3. Organization: Answers are complete and show an understanding of the project.

Score – 3. Accuracy: Information is accurate, but the comments don't go beyond the obvious.

Score – 3. Presentation: Sequenced written work.

Who Am I?

1. I love my family becase I have fun with them

2. I like hockey because it is a thrill to me.

3. I believe in god because I have learned alot about him.

4. Someone I'd like to get to know better is Patrick Roy because Beause he is my favrit hokey player.

5. I have accomplished learning how to ice skate so I could play Ice hockey.

6. I would like to have a million dollers because I could build a huge hose.

7. I appreciate laws so bad people don't hurt use.

8. If I were a teacher I would be a highschool chemistry techer because it would be fun to do all the experimens.

Score – 4. Organization: Each element is addressed with complete understanding of the task.

Score – 4. Accuracy: Writing shows an extended, emotional connection with the audience.

Score – 4. Presentation: Sequenced written work and a quality presentation.

4

MATHEMATICS ACTIVITIES

Mathematics education took on a new look with the National Council of Teachers of Mathematics (NCTM) Standards document written in 1988 and revised in 2000. It was one of the first directives from a national educational organization regarding classroom practices and assessment recommendations. Changes in the use of mathematics, the role of technology, and current research on how students learn best drove the reform movement. The guidelines for the mathematics content taught in schools included input from the business community and international education studies.

The new standards encourage teachers to maintain a balance between the emphasis on conceptual and procedural skills in mathematics. Active student participation in the classroom using a variety of tools for solving problems replaces the previously limited arithmetic curriculum. Paper-and-pencil algorithms are introduced as one way to solve computations. Students who understand the fundamental concepts can retain and expand their knowledge in later years. Repetition is necessary to develop fluency with math facts and can be achieved with motivating, systematic practice with games.

When teachers initiate and maintain a rich cooperative learning environment in which students are encouraged to reason mathematically, ask questions, acknowledge confusion openly, and accept responsibility for helping one another, students will acquire confidence in using mathematics in a meaningful way. Problem solving is not taught as a distinct topic but as a process that permeates the entire mathematics classroom experience. Participating in group projects allows children to immerse themselves in developing their problem-solving abilities while they become part of a team and learn to take another person's perspective.

Tools and technology can encourage student mathematical reasoning. Calculators, computers, concrete materials, visual models, and metaphors can help students express and think about mathematical ideas at a higher level. Resources should be available to provide access to richer learning. This allows students to grapple with more interesting and realistic problems, and helps construct and illustrate their reasoning.

One effective way of learning mathematics is to talk and write about new understandings, relationships, and insights. Writing causes learners to pause and reflect on those connections that consolidate their thoughts.

The new NCTM content standards include the following big ideas:

- **Number and operations** standards guide the development of number sense. Quantities can be counted more efficiently, grouped, combined, and separated. Several of the buddy activities build on estimating and counting by twos, fives, and tens. Other lessons may focus on the relationship between basic operations. Computational fluency, student understanding, and correct record keeping is essential. Counting on and counting backward, looking for patterns in doubles, odd and even number combinations, and thinking in chunks are all strategies for solving problems. It is nearly impossible to do an activity in mathematics that is not related to the number standards. Concrete and visual models with manipulatives provide important insights throughout the elementary school years. Older buddies sometimes understand the mathematical concepts better when they are looking at an actual model of the problem.
- **Algebra** is central to problem solving. During buddy lessons, students work to understand patterns, relations, and functions. Objects, letters and numbers are sorted by color, shape, size, and texture. They are organized and classified in Venn or dichotomous diagrams. Patterns repeat in the lesson, so the students can make generalizations and predict what will happen next. Extended patterns are recursive, and they grow by a predictable amount. Patterns of all kinds allow students to develop confidence with prediction and problem solving. Buddy conversations express algebraic reasoning as students actively build new knowledge from collaborative prior experiences.
- **Geometry** lessons include two- and three-dimensional shapes so that students can describe, model, draw, and classify shapes. Using marshmallows and toothpicks, they investigate and predict the results of combining, subdividing, and changing shapes. Students also relate geometric ideas to number and measurement concepts. They recognize and appreciate geometry in their world through quilts, architecture, and art with symmetry and balance.
- **Measurement** begins with the youngest of children comparing which person is bigger, smaller, or the same size as them. They know which piece of candy they want long before they learn about fractions. Length, weight, capacity, time/duration, circumference, perimeter, and area measurements are high-interest topics for buddy work. Lessons use nonstandard units like cubes, tiles, and string. They are later replaced with standard units of measurement like inches, centimeters, pounds, and liters as the students become more familiar with the need for uniformity. Buddy measurement activities offer many opportunities for students to estimate, solve problems, and demonstrate the integration of number operations skills.

- **Data analysis and probability** standards for primary students include interpreting a variety of picture, symbol, and bar graphs and pie charts. Buddies ask questions, collect the information, create a graph, and record several observations about the statistics. The earliest types of observations students make are "this group has the most" and "this group has the fewest." As students become more proficient, their observations may be based on numeric comparisons like "there are twice as many in this group." The analysis of data takes time and multiple experiences. Advanced students develop and evaluate inferences and predictions that are based on the data. Older buddies follow up and produce tables and charts on the computer to illustrate the information and defend their conclusions.

  Probability is a difficult concept for primary children because they still think the world is fair and they are lucky if they have their favorite shirt on. In any buddy experiment with dice or spinners, some young children pick zero or their age as the winning number regardless of any evidence to the contrary. Just about the time you have them convinced that the statistics would lead to another choice, their lucky number wins! Older students may conclude that the chance of rolling 2 or 12 with two dice is less than the chance of rolling 6, 7, or 8, but it still can happen. Understanding can be a little slippery.
- **Problem solving** is the blending of conceptual and procedural knowledge. Students work on building bridges and relationships among the concepts they are learning. The relationships among measurement, geometry, and number sense standards appear when students are engaged in solving real-world problems. Problems need to be posed on a challenging level mathematically, not just at the students' reading level. Communication, reasoning and proof, connection, and representation are process standards, too. They are the "how" of mathematics instruction and are woven into buddy lesson structures.

When buddy lesson record sheets go home, parents may ask how they can help their children with mathematics. It can be hard not to "tell" children how to do the math even if you want the children to figure it out for themselves. Some of the math may look unfamiliar. Parents can ask questions that will guide their children to discover patterns and relationship in mathematics and the real world. Getting started with questions like "what do you need to find out?" "how might you begin?" and "how can you organize the information?" will support different ways of thinking about a problem. While working with children, parents may want to ask the children to communicate their approach, assumptions, and predictions. Reflecting about the final solution builds confidence in children. They defend their answers with drawings, models, and number operations.

BIRTHDAY CAKE GRAPH

STANDARDS ADDRESSED

- Content: Number & Operations, Measurement, and Data analysis & probability
- Process: Problem solving, communication, connections, and representation

MATERIALS NEEDED

- Birthday cake pattern for each student, copied on two different colors, one color for each grade
- Twelve index cards with the months of the year written on them
- Record sheet for each team
- Scissors and pencils

DIRECTIONS TO THE STUDENTS

Opening: When is your birthday? Do you think other people in this room were born in the same month you were? Do you think there are any other people with your exact same birthday? (A class list may be helpful for the younger children who do not know their birthdays.)

There are two colors of cakes. Older buddies you'll be using _______ cakes. Younger buddies will be using _______ cakes. Cut out your cake and write your name and birthday on it. The months of the year are spelled correctly on a card. Please copy your birth month carefully.

Now let's put them in order. *(Class chants January, February, March, etc.)*

On a large floor area, lay the month cards down one at a time in a circle and have the students with a birthday that month lay their cakes down to the side of the card to create a pie chart. Remember to make the circle large enough for 50 cakes! Someone usually wants to put them in order by birthdate.

Continue with all 12 months. There may be some children with cakes left at the end of your display. Help them find their place.

You may want to correlate the months of the year to the amount of time our earth needs to orbit the sun. A pie graph looks like an orbit.

Have buddy teams talk with each other about something that they noticed about the group data. Share the WOW statements with everyone. Children will notice the colors of cakes, number of birthdays per month, any months that have the same number of cakes, any months that don't have any birthdays, and so on.

Are there two people who have the exact same birthday? What's the probability of that happening, unless you're twins?

Now we'll record our names, birthdates, and best observation statements on the record sheet together.

Wrap up: Have students who finish early check their equations and give each other feedback. They can help collect the cakes to use for a group display.

ASSESSMENT

The record sheet provides an opportunity for students to share their understanding of data analysis. To score an advanced mark (4) on the task, students must compare how many cakes were in each month in relationship to another month. They may see that one month has only younger buddies' birthdays. Some students may count all the cakes and make statements that express the fractional equivalence of a subgroup. The group discussions model what we're looking for in observation statements.

CAKE PATTERN

BIRTHDAY CAKES

My name is ____

My buddy's name is ____

I was born in ____

My buddy was born in ______________________________________

Two things we noticed about our group pie chart are ________________

____

____

____

____

____

BUYING BOOKS

STANDARDS ADDRESSED

- Content: Number & Operations and Measurement
- Process: Problem solving, communication, reasoning, and proof

MATERIALS NEEDED

- Book orders from any book club company
- Record sheet
- Pencils
- Calculators

DIRECTIONS TO THE STUDENTS

Opening: Have you ever ordered books from a club? About how much do you pay for each book? What chores can you do around the house to earn some money of your own to buy books?

We will pretend that you and your buddy have just received some allowance money. You each got the amount of your exact age right now. How much will you have to spend all together? Estimate how many books can you buy all together.

Now look at the book order form. Find a book you'd each like to buy. Record the name of the books on the record sheet. Round the book prices to the nearest dollar and continue to estimate your spending. Spend as close to the dollar amount you have, but remember, you can't spend more than you have.

The younger buddy will add the approximate total cost of the books chosen. The older buddy will add up the total cost of the actual prices. Compare your results. Was your rounding close?

Now check your work with a calculator. Show your buddies how to use the calculator keys and coach them through the process. How much money did you have left over? Is there any other combination of books that would work for your solution? How do you know?

Wrap up: When did you know it was time to quit shopping? When else do you use rounding in your life?

ASSESSMENT

The record sheet provides an opportunity for students to share their learning. To score an advanced mark (4) on the task, students must expand the mathematical concepts beyond the obvious and offer multiple solutions to a problem. This activity can be adapted for second- through sixth-grade work depending on the student's proficiency with addition computation, with and without regrouping. Encourage students to use the dollar and cents notation.

BUYING BOOKS WITH MY BUDDY

Names ____

How old are you? __________ How old is your buddy? __________

How much money will you pretend to have all together to spend on books?

____

Look at the book order form. Estimate how many books you can purchase with that amount. We think we can get ______________ books.

Have the younger buddy keep track of about how much you've spent by rounding each book cost to the nearest dollar. Remember the goal is to spend as much of your money as you can *without going over* the amount you have. Record the names of the books you want to buy and the prices you'll have to pay. Have the older buddy add up the actual cost of all the books together and show your work.

Name of book	*About how much*	*Actual cost*
	TOTAL	TOTAL

Did you have any money left over? ________ How much? ______________

You may check your work with a calculator. Record the steps you took to solve this problem on the back of this record sheet.

How old are you? 8 How old is your buddy? 12

How much money will you pretend to have all together, to spend on books? $20.00

Look at the book order form. Estimate how many books you can purchase. We can get about _____ books.

Round each item to the nearest dollar. Have the younger buddy keep track of how much you've spent. Remember the goal is to spend as much of your money as you can <u>without going over</u> the amount you have. Record the names of the books you want to buy and the prices you'll have to pay. Have the older buddy add up all the books together and show your work.

Name of book	About how much	Actual cost
Britney Spears	$3.00	$2.95
Live [illegible]	$3.00	$2.95
N SYNC	[illegible]	[illegible]
It's fine to be (Mine!)	3.00	2.95
Halloween	2.00	1.95
Scooby [illegible]	3.00	$2.95
[illegible]	3.00	$2.95
and [illegible]	3.00	$2195
	TOTAL	

Did you have any money left over? How much? __________

You may **check** your work with a calculator.

Write the steps you took to solve this problem.

Cloudy With a Chance of Meatballs

$3.95

$6 \times 3 = 18$

Score – 2. Organization: Omitted estimate and total of books purchased.

Score – 2. Accuracy: Information is mostly accurate. Project was not completed. There is $20 worth of books listed, but the final amount wasn't recorded and the amount of money left over.

Score – 1. Presentation: No explanation or solution is given. Even with additional time, this team did not complete the task.

How old are you? 9 How old is your buddy? 11
How much money will you pretend to have all together, to spend on books? $20
Look at the book order form. Estimate how many books you can purchase. We can get about 8 books.

Round each item to the nearest dollar. Have the younger buddy keep track of how much you've spent. Remember the goal is to spend as much of your money as you can <u>without going over</u> the amount you have. Record the names of the books you want to buy and the prices you'll have to pay. Have the older buddy add up all the books together and show your work.

Name of book	About how much	Actual cost
National Geographic	$5.00	$4.95
Science	$1.00	$.95
Guinness	$5.00	$4.95
Goblins Don't Play Video Games	$2.00	$1.95
Secrets of Droon	$1.00	$.95
N Sync/Five	$3.00	$2.95
Brittany Spears	$3.00	$2.95
	TOTAL	19.65

Did you have any money left over? How much? $0.35
You may **check** your work with a calculator.
Write the steps you took to solve this problem.

1. Round
2. Add Actual cost
3 check with calculator

Score – 3. Organization: Understands the problem and the work is completed.
Score – 3. Accuracy: Estimates book costs, and remaining money is accurate and complete.
Score – 3. Presentation: Written works is brief, but sequenced correctly.

How old are you? 11 How old is your buddy? 8

How much money will you pretend to have all together, to spend on books? $19

$11 + 8 = 19$

Look at the book order form. Estimate how many books you can purchase. We can get about 8 books.

Round each item to the nearest dollar. Have the younger buddy keep track of how much you've spent. Remember the goal is to spend as much of your money as you can without going over the amount you have. Record the names of the books you want to buy and the prices you'll have to pay. Have the older buddy add up all the books together and show your work.

Name of book	About how much	Actual cost
Tricked or Treats	$5.00	$4.95
There was An Old...	$4.00	$3.95
The 13 Night of Halloween	$3.00	$2.95
Mouse/Manners Book	$4.00	$3.95
Peptalk Surprise	$3.00	$2.50
	$19.00	

TOTAL $18.30

$19.00 − 18.30 = $0.70

First we figured out how much money we had all together

Did you have any money left over? How much? $0.70

You may **check** your work with a calculator.

Write the steps you took to solve this problem.

First we looked at books, then we decided what books we liked. Ashley picked a book, then [illegible] wrote the name and actual cost, then Ashley estimated the price. Ashley added the estimates, then [illegible] added the actual prices. Ashley and [illegible] subtracted $18.30 from $19.00 to

WOW!!

Score – 3. Organization: Elements are present but a little difficult to follow.

Score – 4. Accuracy: Calculation is accurate and task is complete.

Score – 4. Presentation: Used complete sentences and lots of details in the written explanation of the project. Evidence of cooperative team work.

DICHOTOMOUS CLASSIFICATION

STANDARDS ADDRESSED

- Content: Algebra and Data analysis & probability
- Process: Problem solving, communication, reasoning, proof, and representation

Comment: This is a great activity to put together during the holidays when the candy variety is easily found for a good price. Dichotomous classification can be used to sort science objects or pictures of animals, plants, habitats, five senses, solar system, etc. Social studies units with postcards and pictures of land, air and water transportation, careers, continents, needs and wants, etc., can be used, too. The applications are endless.

MATERIALS NEEDED

- One small sandwich bag with a variety of candies, wrapped, unwrapped, chocolate, nonchocolate, fruit, soft, and hard kinds for each team of buddies
- Blank sheet of paper 11×17 inches
- 11×17-inch graphic organizer for sorting
- Pencils and crayons

DIRECTIONS TO THE STUDENTS

Opening: What do you think the word *dichotomous* means? Do you know what *di* means? (Two.) Dichotomous classification means we will sort the candies into two, and only two, groups at one time.

Today we will estimate how many candies are in our bag. Record your guess and your buddy's. Now dump the candy out of the bag and count out the pieces in groups of tens and ones so that it is easier to skip count by tens. Compare your estimates to the actual amount. Whose estimate was the closest?

Now put your candy in the circle at the top of the graphic organizer. Label your collection. How will your team sort the candy? Label the next two circles and sort the candies into those two attributes. Every piece of candy needs to be in one of the circles. You can choose chocolate and nonchocolate, but not chocolate, mint, and fruit because that would be three groups.

Continue to sort your collection in two groups until you've completed the graphic organizer. Label your groups each time and remember to keep the sorted candy separate from the other sorting groups.

Complete the record sheet with your buddy. What did you notice about the groups you sorted? Which group has the most? Which group had the least?

Wrap up: Have students who finish early share their sorting strategies with each other and give each other feedback.

ASSESSMENT

The record sheet and sorting organizer provide an opportunity for students to demonstrate their understanding about classification. To score an advanced mark (4) on the task, students must expand the dichotomous classification concept. This activity can be adapted for first- through sixth-grade work depending on the written work expected of the younger buddy. Sorting in two categories can be challenging for students that want to sort in colors, sizes, and shapes. Refocus those teams that get off track right away.

DICHOTOMOUS CLASSIFICATION

Names ____

1. We estimated the candies in our bag.

   My buddy's guess ______________ My guess ______________

   Actual count ______________

   Compare the three numbers. ______________________________

____

____

2. Today we sorted holiday candies in many different ways. Dichotomous

means ____

____

3. When my buddy and I sorted our candy, we noticed ______________

____

____

____

4. Three statements that describe our sorting arrangements are __________

____

____

____

____

5. Other things we could sort this way are ______________________

____

____

#1. We estimated the candies in our bag.

My buddy's guess 30 My guess 45

Actual count 52

Compare the three numbers. Kevin's guess was 45 Kody's guess was 30

#2. Today we sorted holiday candies in many different ways.

Dichotomous means Dichotomous means you divide.

3. When my buddy and I sorted our candy, we noticed we had more mints.

4. Three statements that describe our sorting arrangements are

It was fun.

Hard in some places.

And neat to do.

#5. Other things we could sort this way would be ________

Score – 2. Organization: Omitted labeling in the third and fourth row on the sorting organizer. Does not show a complete understanding of the problem.

Score – 1. Accuracy: Project is partially completed with inaccurate conclusions about dichotomous classification.

Score – 1. Presentation: Incomplete communication about estimation, comparisons, and application of sorting.

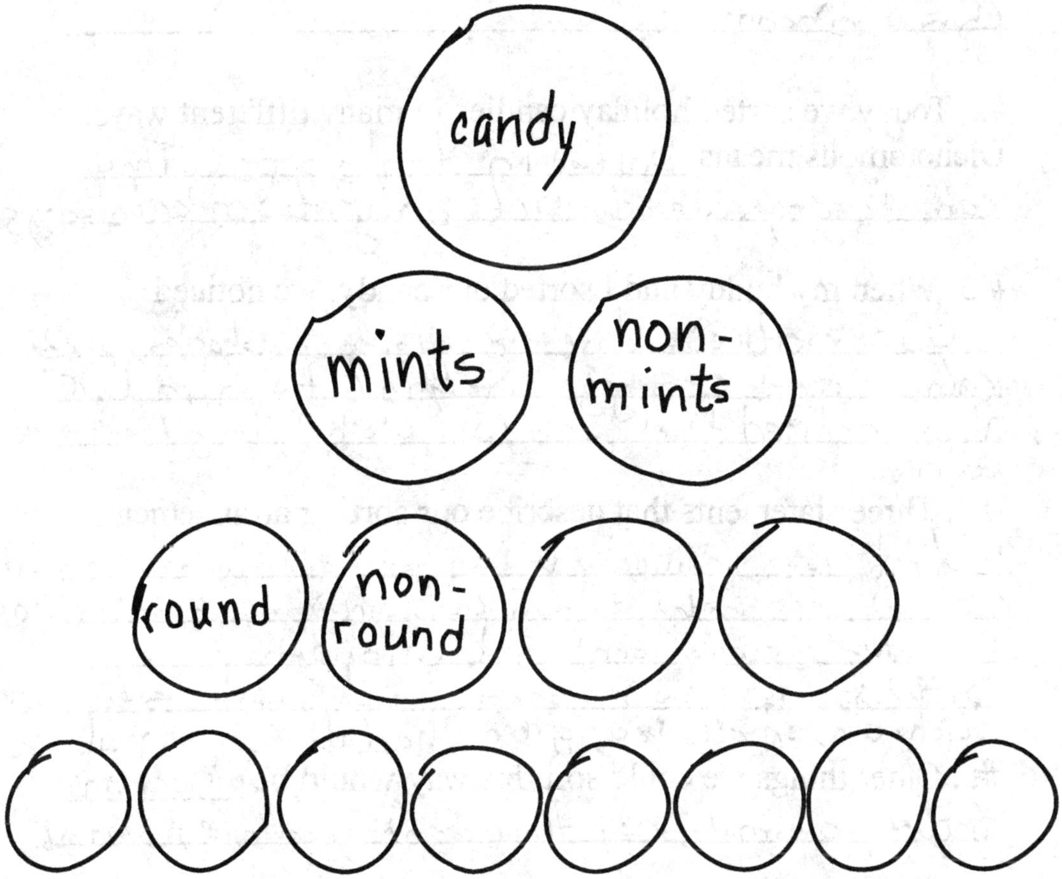
candy
mints
non-mints
round
non-round

#1. We estimated the candies in our bag.

My buddy's guess 40 My guess 45

Actual count 68

Compare the three numbers. Johanna was 28 less I was 23 less. I guessed 45, 5 more than Johanna

68 −40 = 28 | 68 −45 = 23

#2. Today we sorted holiday candies in many different ways. Dichotomous means Sorted in to groups. They can be any category but only two categorys per

3. When my buddy and I sorted our candy, we noticed We noticed the different shapes, sizes, colors and categorys we put them in. We also noticed the way we worked to gether as a team.

4. Three statements that describe our sorting arrangements are

1. first we divided them in to mints and not mints
2. Second we sorted them in to swirled in middle, not swirled in middle, wrapped and not wrapped.
3. Second we divided them in to: with stick, with out stick, big, small, red, green, choclate and not choclate

#5. Other things we could sort this way would be humans, papers, animals, hair things and sports equipment

---

Score – 3. Organization: Shows an understanding of the classification task.

Score – 4. Accuracy: Estimate comparison is clearly explained and multiple observations are correct.

Score – 4. Presentation: Detailed explanation about sorting process and application of the process. #3 Team also noticed they were "working together to learn."

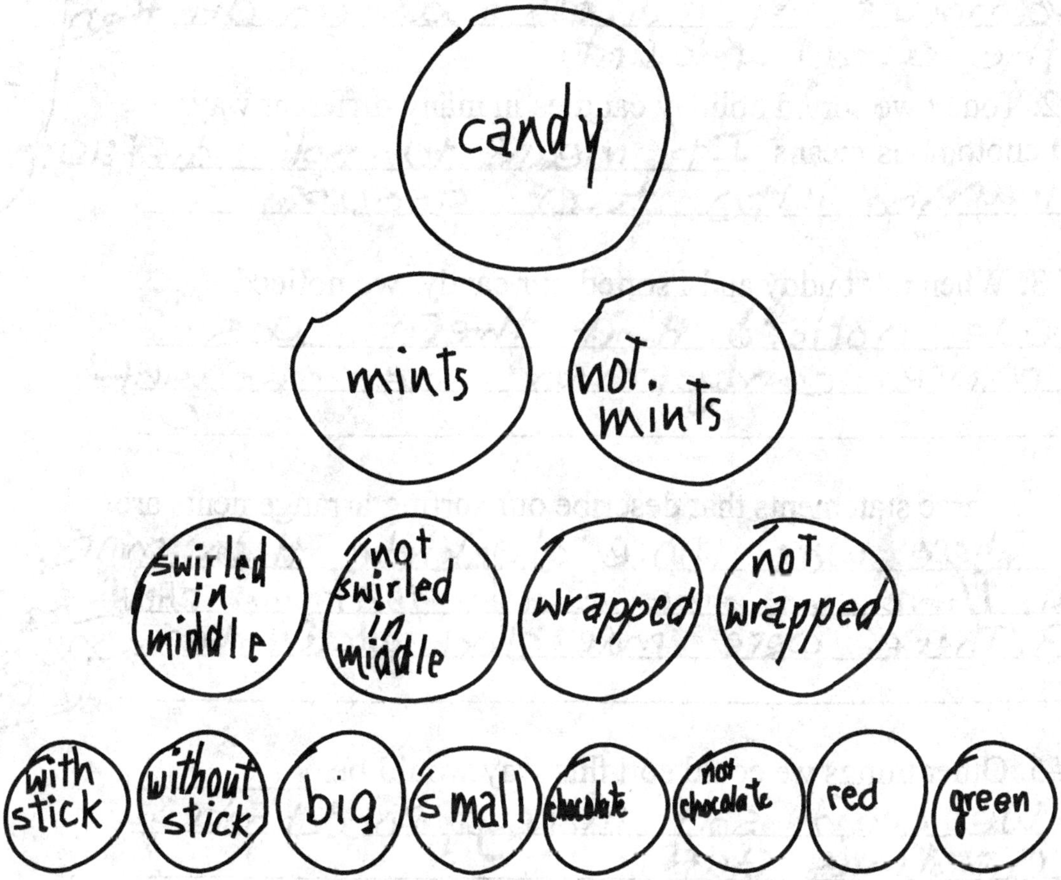
candy
mints
not. mints
swirled in middle
not swirled in middle
wrapped
not wrapped
with stick
without stick
big
small
chocolate
not chocolate
red
green

#1. We estimated the candies in our bag.

My buddy's guess 30 My guess 20

Actual count 80

Compare the three numbers. My buddies guess was 50 off than the actail amount. My guess was 60 off than the actal amount.

80
-30
50

80
-20
60

#2. Today we sorted holiday candies in many different ways.

Dichotomous means It means to split different thangs into two groups.

3. When my buddy and I sorted our candy, we noticed we noticed that there was more candy than we thought

4. Three statements that describe our sorting arrangements are

1. There was more chocklete than mints.
2. There was more candy that you chew-on than suck.
3. There were more chocklete than any other.
4.

#5. Other things we could sort this way would be We could sort money, food, books & christmas stuff.

Score – 4. Organization: Elements are clearly represented on the organizer with a complete understanding of the dichotomous sorting process.

Score – 3. Accuracy: Information is accurate and project is complete.

Score – 4. Presentation: Written work and visual model communicates the sorting task elegantly.

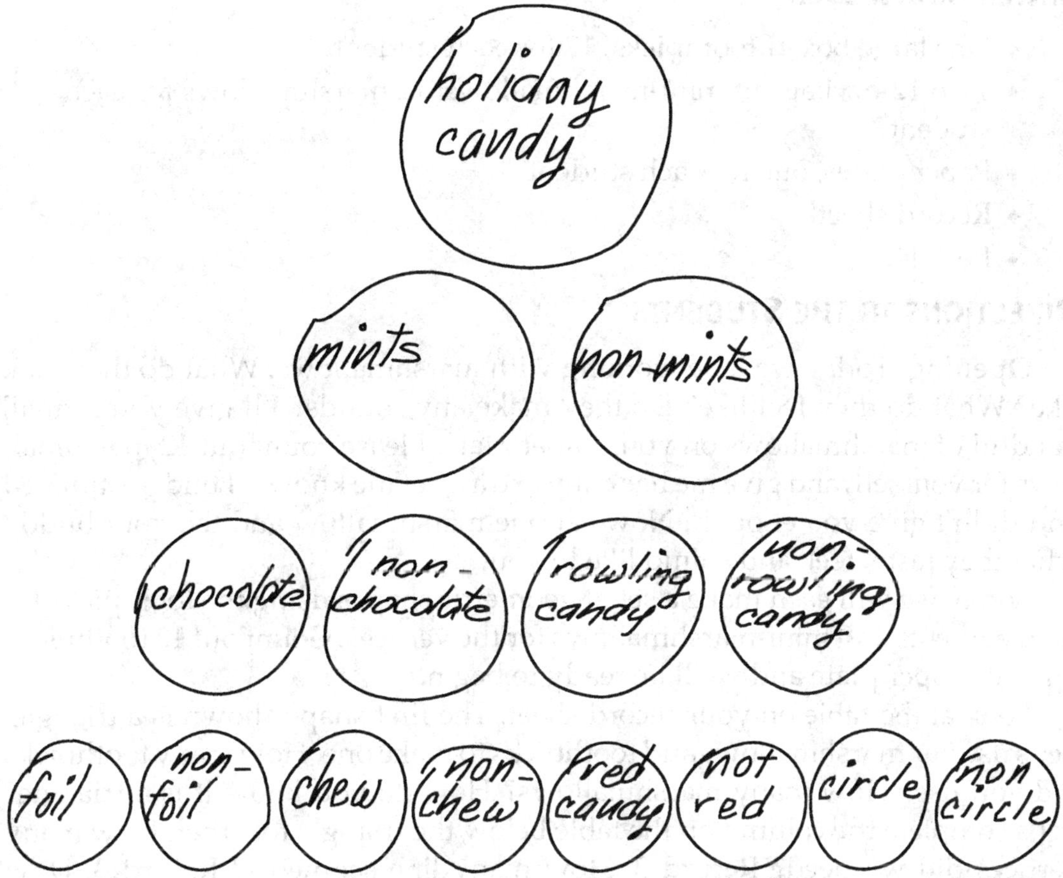
holiday candy
mints
non-mints
chocolate
non-chocolate
rowling candy
non-rowling candy
foil
non-foil
chew
non-chew
red candy
not red
circle
non circle

GEO-MALLOWS

STANDARDS ADDRESSED

- Content: Number & operations and Geometry
- Process: Problem solving, communication, and representation

MATERIALS NEEDED

- One large box of toothpicks, 12 for each student
- Two 12-oz. bags of mini-marshmallows; 12 marshmallows for each student
- Paper plates, one for each student
- Record sheet
- Pencils

DIRECTIONS TO THE STUDENTS

Opening: Today we'll be working with marshmallows. What do they look like? What do they feel like? Do they make any sounds? I'll give you a small handful of marshmallows on your paper plate. Please count out 12 marshmallows for yourself, and give me back any extras. Let me know if I underestimated and didn't give you enough. Now eat one marshmallow and tell your buddy what they taste, feel, and sound like to you.

Today we will each make a set of geometric shapes using the toothpicks for line segments and mini-marshmallows for the vertices. Count out 12 toothpicks on your paper plate and we'll be ready to begin.

Look at the table on your record sheet. The first shape shown is a triangle. Let's use our marshmallows and toothpicks to make one. How many toothpicks did you use? How many marshmallows? How do you know it is a triangle? Let's complete the column on the table below the triangle together. How many vertices did we need? Record 3. How many line segments? Record 3. How many faces or sides does a triangle have? Record 1. (Students may generate a discussion about one dimensional versus two dimensional shapes. You may want to defer to your math program for vocabulary and definitions, so that the lesson is consistent with your class work.)

Now let's make a square. Can you use some of the toothpicks and marshmallows from your triangle shape? Check your buddy's work. Do they need some help?

Let's count the number of vertices, the number of line segments and the faces together and record them on the sheet. What do you notice about the first two shapes?

You'll continue with the remaining shapes in the table. What's different about them? Work together and actually build each shape. Count the vertices, segments and faces together with your buddy. Record you work.

When you have completed the activity, write at least one statements about something you learned.

Wrap up: Some students may finish early. Have them build a different 3D figure of their own and record the same information. Then have all the students check their record sheet for correct answers and share their best observations with each other. They may eat the marshmallows and throw away the toothpicks and paper plates.

ASSESSMENT

The record sheet provides an opportunity for students to communicate their understanding of geometric shapes, vertices, segments and faces. Once students have built these one and three dimensional shapes they really can SEE the relationship between vertices, segments and faces. To score an advanced (4) on the task, students must expand the concept of geometry beyond the task. This activity can be adapted for first through sixth grade work depending on the vocabulary and algorithms introduced.

GEO-MALLOWS ACTIVITY SHEET

Names

Build these shapes with toothpicks and mini-marshmallows. Fill in the chart below.

Shapes	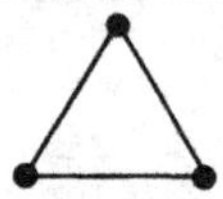	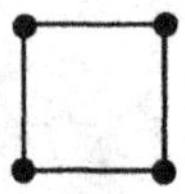	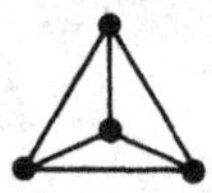	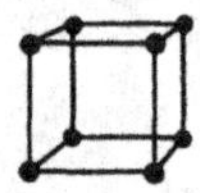	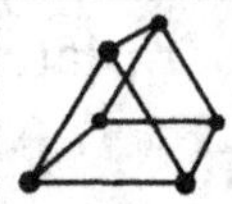	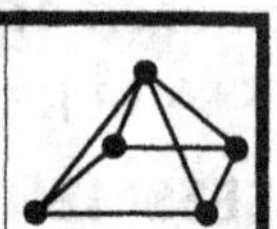
# of points/ vertices (marshmallows)						
# of line segments/edges (toothpicks)						
# of faces (sides)						

What Do You Notice?

GUESSING ABOUT CAPACITY

STANDARDS ADDRESSED

- Content: Number & operations and Measurement
- Process: Problem solving, communication, and representation

MATERIALS NEEDED

- A collection of 50 to 100 varied items like shells, coins, keys, beads, macaroni, nuts, bolts and screws, barrettes, pom-poms, buttons, tiles, cubes, and blocks for each team of buddies
- Record sheet for each team or one for each grade 3–6 student
- Pencils

DIRECTIONS TO THE STUDENTS

Opening: Where have you seen the word *capacity*? Students may answer: a restaurant, the school gym, a school bus, swimming pool, and/or a theatre. What does it mean? Why is it important? Visualize what happens when you pour some cereal into a bowl, up to the top. Then you add milk. What happens?

We are going to use your hand capacity to grab different objects. Compare your hand to your buddy's. Whose hand is larger? Whose hand will hold more objects? Let's see what happens.

Record the name of the items you will grab. Estimate how many items you think you will be able to hold in your hand. Have your partner estimate how many he/she will be able to grab. Take turns grabbing and counting out the objects in groups of tens, and then record your actual amounts. Write a comparison statement about your estimates and your hand capacities.

Then go on to another collection of items. Continue until you and your buddy have measured your capacity with four different items.

Wrap up: Have students who finish early share their observations with each other.

ASSESSMENT

The record sheet provides an opportunity for students to share their understanding of estimation and measurement. To score an advanced mark (4) on the task, students must expand the mathematical concept of capacity to show a complete understanding. This activity can be adapted for first- through sixth-grade work depending on the quantities used in the collections and the expectation for math vocabulary used in the comparison statements.

GUESSING ABOUT CAPACITY WITH MY BUDDY

Names____

My buddy and I are going to guess about four items. We will each *estimate* how many treasures we can grab with one hand. We will *count* the number of objects in our hand and record the actual number. Then we will *compare* the amounts.

Name of item	*Our estimates*		*Our actual count*	

Compare: ____

Name of item	*Our estimates*		*Our actual count*	

Compare: ____

Name of item	*Our estimates*		*Our actual count*	

Compare: ____

Name of item	*Our estimates*		*Our actual count*	

Compare: ____

My buddy and I are going to guess about four items. We will each **estimate** how many treasures we can grab with one hand. We will **count** the number of objects in our hand and record the actual number. Then we will **compare** the amounts.

Name of item	my estimate	actual count
hair pins	21 | 22	27 | 36

Compare: Leif guessed 21 He picked up 36

Name of item	my estimate	actual count
niles	70 | 27	20 | 24

Compare: CoreyB guessed 27 I picked up 20.

Name of item	my estimate	actual count
Tees	79 | 2	44 | 47

Compare: Leif guessed 79 He picked up 44.

Name of item	my estimate	actual count
pompoms	79 | 44	40 | 38

Compare: ______________________

Score – 2. Organization: Missing elements indicate lack of understanding with comparison statements.

Score – 1. Accuracy: Information is incomplete and does not include comparing statements, but a repeat of the obvious.

Score – 1. Presentation: No explanation was given for the difference in numerals and the team did not complete the work.

My buddy and I are going to guess about four items. We will each **estimate** how many treasures we can grab with one hand. We will **count** the number of objects in our hand and record the actual number. Then we will **compare** the amounts.

Name of item	my estimate	actual count
macaroni	50	42

Compare: I have 4 less that Jacob.

Name of item	my estimate	actual count
round things	20	14

Compare: I had 2 more than Jacob.

Name of item	my estimate	actual count
tiles	25	27

Compare: I had 7 more than Jacob.

Name of item	my estimate	actual count
nuts, bolts, etc.	27	62

Compare: I had 11 more than Jacob.

Score – 3. Organization: These two buddies worked on separate papers. Estimates and comparing statements are present.

Score – 3. Accuracy: Statements show an understanding of the comparing process and estimates are mostly accurate, too.

Score – 3. Presentation: Written work indicates a sequenced approach.

My buddy and I are going to guess about four items. We will each **estimate** how many treasures we can grab with one hand. We will **count** the number of objects in our hand and record the actual number. Then we will **compare** the amounts.

Name of item	my estimate		actual count	
Sea shells	6	10	14	8

Compare: I had 4 more than Caitlin.

Name of item	my estimate		actual count	
Nuts and bolts	20	15	11	36

Compare: Caitlin had 25 less than me.

Name of item	my estimate		actual count	
barrettes	20	37	22	41

Compare: I had 19 more then Caitlin

Name of item	my estimate		actual count	
golf tees	30	45	32	62

Compare: Caitlin had 31 less than me.

Score – 4. Organization: Team worked efficiently with task and recorded additional work on the back of the record sheet.

Score – 4. Accuracy: Accurate comparing statements alternated between more and less comparisons.

Score – 4. Presentation: Elegant and exemplary explanation about what capacity is and where you would use it.

1. Capacity is when there is not enough room to move.

2. In a pool you need enough room to swim thats also capacity.

3. Older people have more capacity in there hands.

4. In Apple Bees can only be so many people.

ME AND MY BUDDY GLYPHS

This is an excellent first lesson for buddies to get to know each other. It can be extended for two sessions.

STANDARDS ADDRESSED

- Content: Algebra and Data analysis & probability
- Process: Problem solving, communication, reasoning, proof, and representation

MATERIALS NEEDED

- Pattern of an object for each student (see bat pattern)
- Any science or social studies theme
- Record sheet for each team
- Legend of directions for coloring in the glyph object
- Two hula hoops, index cards, marker
- Pencils and crayons

DIRECTIONS TO THE STUDENTS

Opening: To set the stage, choose a book that goes along with your basic theme pattern, to read together or as individual classes.

Have your ever heard of a glyph? What word does it sound like? (Hieroglyphics, a picture representation that conveys information.) What do you know about glyphs? Have you ever made one? What did you learn?

Today we will follow specific directions to decorate our personal glyph, so that all of our pictures will be made according to the same attributes. Then we will sort, classify, and describe ourselves by the attributes on the legend. *(The "making" part of the lesson will take approximately 15 minutes. Suggestions for attributes are included in this lesson, but frequently the children will generate their own ideas. While you're waiting for everyone to finish, begin a discussion with the students who have completed their work around a large floor space.)*

How could we sort our glyphs into groups? Students suggest attributes from the legend. Let's put the _____ in this group and the _____ in this one. These can go here. *(Teacher helps student's arrange their glyphs in a bar graph display. Label each sorting category with an index card.)* Which group has more? How do you know? What else do you notice? *(Encourage students to make numeric comparisons.)*

Comment: Depending on the experience level of the students participating, graphing extensions may take more or less time. Try to sort and graph in at least two different ways. Gauge your group's attention for this part of the lesson by their on-task behavior and interest in sorting their glyphs. The other teacher present can record some of the verbal observations students are contributing to use with a wall display later.

Continue this part of the lesson if you have time or begin the next session here.

The students can play Detective Glyph for a warm up. Choose one glyph from the group. Hold it up and ask students to sit down, one attribute at a time, if this glyph doesn't represent who they are. For instance: Sit down if you have more than one syllable in your name. Sit down if you like bats. Sit down if you like pumpkin pie or candy corn. The final remaining person should be the owner of the glyph. Sometimes there are two or three students left standing, and you have to ask other clues not related to the glyph legend, like "Did you use crayon on your picture?" The students really enjoy this game and won't tell who it is even if they know! Play Detective Glyph at least twice and then begin the second part of the lesson.

Last time we made bar graphs with our glyphs by sorting them into several different categories. This time let's use these hoops. Use one card from one sorting group (e.g., older buddies) and place the label by the hula hoop. Have the students put their glyphs into the hoop if it applies. Select another card from the other sorting group (e.g., have two syllables in their names) and have all the students place their glyph inside the second hoop if it applies. *Inevitably someone will belong to both groups, and you'll have a problem. Ask for suggestions from the group. Place one hoop over the top of the other to create an overlapping area. This is a powerful visual model of a Venn diagram.*

What will we do with the other glyphs? *The teacher may want to suggest that the collection outside the hoops does not belong to either group and therefore is "outside the sorting set."*

What's another way we could sort these glyphs? *(Model the Venn diagram classification another way if time and interest allow.)*

Now each buddy team is ready to complete the record sheet provided. First the younger buddy will write three clues from the legend about who they are. For instance: I am eight. I like evenings. My name has two syllables. Then the older buddy will complete three clues. On the back of the record sheet, the buddies will compare and contrast their glyphs using the Venn diagram model.

Wrap up: Have the students who finish early give each other feedback about shared attributes and observation statements.

When the buddy group has completed the glyph lesson, attach the collection of glyphs to a wall display using a bar graph or Venn diagram format. Include a legend, the observations from the group discussions, and a title.

ASSESSMENT

The record sheet provides an opportunity for students to share their understanding of classification and comparisons. To score an advanced mark (4) on the task, students must write at least three clues and record a complex interpretation of the data, using fractions and well-developed mathematical vocabulary. This activity can be adapted for first- through sixth-grade work by limiting or expanding the number of attributes in the legend. Early in the year, older buddies may have to write all the clues and ideas. This activity can be repeated several times during the year using various themes. Students can revisit their previous learning and expand their understanding of the concepts.

ME AND MY BUDDY GLYPHS

Names____

Glyphs are pictures that represent certain attributes. We've used them today to sort, classify, and describe ourselves as a group. Now it's your turn to work with just your glyph and your buddy's.

Write three clues that would give someone an idea of who you are based on the attributes we used today.

____

____

____

____

Write three clues that would give someone an idea of who your buddy is based on the attributes we used today.

____

____

____

____

On the back of this paper use the Venn diagram to compare and contrast your attributes with your buddy's.

BAT GLYPH PATTERN

BAT GLYPH LEGEND

Bat wing color

Yellow	My name has 1 syllable.
Orange	My name has 2 syllables.
Brown	My name has 3 or more syllables.

Smile

Happy Face	I have a costume.
Sad Face	I don't have a costume.
Straight Line	I don't need a costume.

Eyes

△	I like candy corn.
○	I like pumpkin pie.
□	I like popcorn balls.

Vertical stripes on the wing represent my age.

Moon

Full	I am a younger buddy.
Crescent	I am an older buddy.

BUDDY GLYPH VENN DIAGRAM

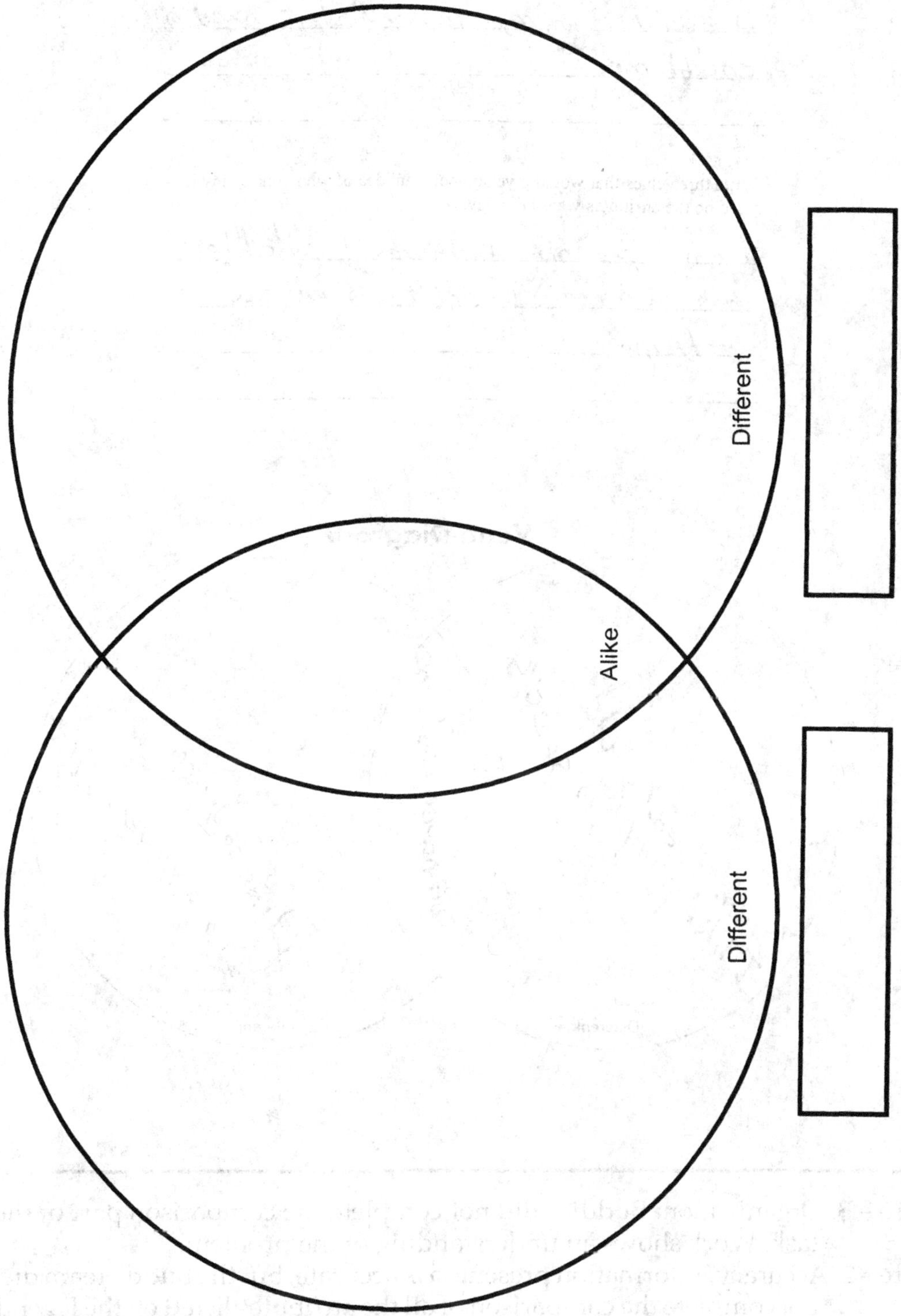

I am 9 years old. And I have 2 sylables in my name. And I need a costhme.

Write three clues that would give someone an idea of who your buddy is based on the attributes we used today.

I am 6 year old. I have 3 sylables in my name. I don't need a costume.

Venn Diagram

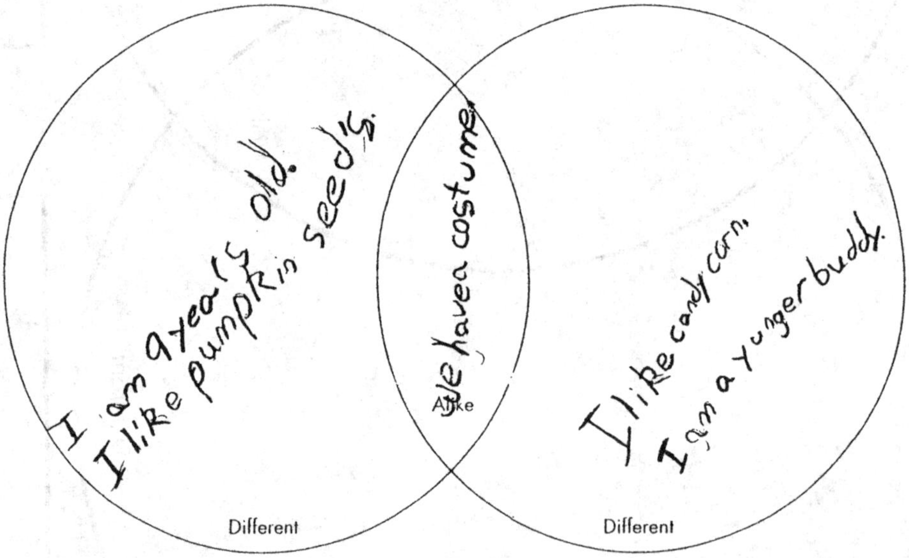

Score – 3. Organization: Buddies did not complete the comparison part of the task. Work shows an understanding of the problem.

Score – 2. Accuracy: Information presented is accurate, but the buddy team did not complete the comparison of all the attributes listed on the legend.

Score – 2. Presentation: Team did use complete sentences for their statements, however, they did not compare all the glyph elements.

Write three clues that would give someone an idea of who you are based on the attributes we used today.

I am an older buddy.
I like pumpkin pie.
I have two syllables in my name.

Write three clues that would give someone an idea of who your buddy is based on the attributes we used today.

I like pumpkin pie.
I have two syllables in my name.
I am a younger buddy.

Venn Diagram

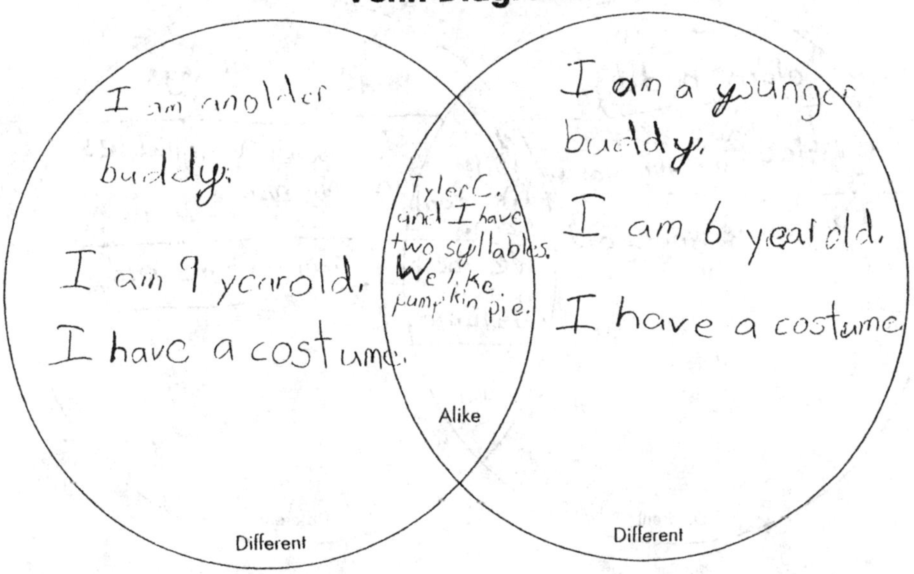

Score – 4. Organization: All the elements are clearly presented. Work shows an understanding of the Venn diagram.

Score – 3. Accuracy: Comparisons of all the attributes on the glyph legend are complete and accurate.

Score – 3. Presentation: Team used complete sentences in their work, but did not expand on the task.

I am an older buddy.
I have 3 syllables in my name.
I have a costume.
I like candy corn.

Write three clues that would give someone an idea of who your buddy is based on the attributes we used today.

I am a younger buddy.
I have 2 syllables in my name.
I have a costume.
I like candy corn.

Venn Diagram

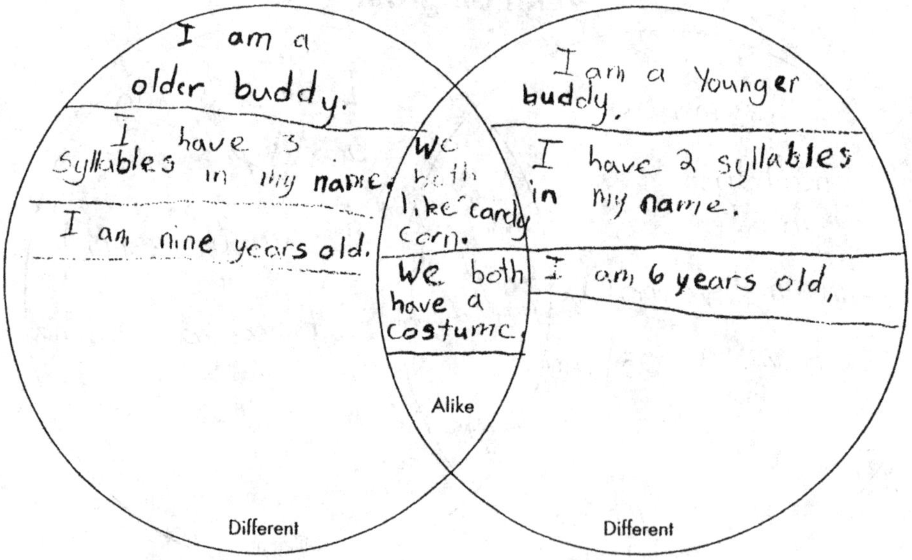

Score – 4. Organization: All the elements are clearly presented in complete sentences with capital letters and correct spelling of most high frequency words.
Score – 3. Accuracy: Information is accurate and complete.
Score – 4. Presentation: Team wrote four sentences to describe who they are, but only dealt with the legend attributes for the Venn diagram.

MENU MATH

STANDARDS ADDRESSED

- Content: Number & operations and Measurement
- Process: Problem solving, communication, connections, and representation

MATERIALS NEEDED

- Adult menus, or copies, from local restaurants, one per team
- Record sheet for each team
- Calculators, at least one for every four students
- Pencils

DIRECTIONS TO THE STUDENTS

Opening: About how much do you think it costs to go to a restaurant with your family for dinner? (*Teachers may want to record the number of people in the student's family and their estimate amounts for a comparison. This activity can easily be expanded to a lesson on averages.*)

How old are you? How old is your buddy? Add that amount together and that's how much you'll pretend to have to spend on dinner for the two of you. Look at the menu. Find some of your favorite foods. What can you both order so that you'll be sure to have enough money? Record the item and the cost on the record sheet provided.

This lesson can be made more challenging for buddies by asking students to compute the state tax and a 15% tip.

Calculators are used to check their computation work. You may need to encourage the older buddy to coach the younger buddy through the process of using a calculator. Note: Inexperienced students are surprised by the disappearing zero on the calculator screen.

Complete the remaining questions on your record sheet with your buddy.

Wrap up: Have students who finish early share their observations with each other. Is there more than one way to solve this type of problem? What else could you have bought? Were there teams that had more money? What did they spend it on? About how much would it cost for your family if you used this menu?

ASSESSMENT

The record sheet provides an opportunity for students to share their understanding of addition and subtraction concepts, money, and percentages. To score an advanced mark (4) on the task, students must extend the application to averages or connect this activity with their real life. This activity can be adapted for third- through sixth-grade work depending on the computation standards for the grade levels involved.

> **After this activity, parents have enthusiastically reported the interest in which their child calculates the family meal totals, tax, *and* tip in a restaurant. Their child appreciates the cost of family dinners out and the importance of quality service.**

MENU MATH RECORD SHEET

Names ____

How old are you? ________ How old is your buddy? ________ Add that amount together. ________ You will pretend you have *that much money* to spend at *a restaurant*. You may choose any combination of items on the menu. You must have enough for a 15% tip and 5% tax. You may use a calculator to check your work. What will you order?

Item	*Cost*
Subtotal	
Tax	
Tip	
Total	

What operations did you use to solve this problem? What estimation skills did you use?

How much money will you have left over? ________________

What else did you learn?

ODD AND EVEN, FAIR GAME

STANDARDS ADDRESSED

- Content: Number & operations, Algebra, and Data analysis & probability
- Process: Problem solving, communication, and representation

MATERIALS NEEDED

- A pair of regular six-sided dice for each team
- Paper with lines for each team
- Pencils

DIRECTIONS TO THE STUDENTS

Opening: 2, 4, 6, 8, 10, 12. What do those numerals have in common? Share your ideas with your buddy. What's my rule? What would the next numeral be in the sequence? How do you know? These are all even numbers.

If I am counting 1, 3, 5, 7, 9, 11, 13, what's my pattern? Let's team up with another buddy group and see what ideas you all have. Yes, these numerals are all odd numbers.

Today we will take turns rolling the two dice. I will roll for the younger buddies, Player A. I rolled a 4 and a 3; 4 + 3 +7. Player A scores a point if the sum is even. Is the numeral 7 odd or even? How do you know?

Player B scores a point if the sum is odd. This time the older buddies will get a point because 7 is an odd number. Let's make a record sheet. Fold your paper in half vertically. Label the left side <u>Player A Even</u> and the right side <u>Player B Odd</u>. I will record my equation under their column.

Now it's the older buddies' turn. Their teacher will roll. He gets a 6 and a 1; 6 + 1 = 7. Seven is an odd number, so the equation is written in the Player B column. So far, B is ahead!

Let's roll one more time. This time I got a 2 and another 2; 2 + 2 = 4. Four is an even number, so the equation is written in the Player A column.

You and your buddy will roll 20 times. Each time you roll, decide if the sum is an odd or even number and write the complete equation under the correct column. Odd numbers are under Player B; even numbers, under Player A. Stop at 20 rolls.

Is this game "fair"? Why or why not?

How could you make the game "fair"?

Wrap up: Have students who finish early share their data results and analysis. Which came up most often, odd or even, and why? Would there be any way of rewriting the game rules so that the game could be fair?

ASSESSMENT

The written record provides an opportunity for students to organize and collect data, practice basic facts, and communicate the relationship of odd and even number patterns. To score an advanced mark (4) on the task, students must complete one game with their buddy and suggest alternative rules to make this game "fair." This activity can be adapted for fourth- through sixth-grade work by changing the operation to multiplication. If the product is even, Player A scores. If the product is odd, Player B scores the point. Students look for patterns and the relationship between even and odd numbers in multiplication. They can compare the results of their addition game to their multiplication game. Are there rules that would make the multiplication game "fair"?

PAPER QUILTS

STANDARDS ADDRESSED

- Content: Geometry and Measurement
- Process: Problem solving, connections, and representation

MATERIALS NEEDED

- 1-inch squares cut from construction paper, in two or three colors: for example, your school colors; orange, yellow, and brown in the fall; or red, white, and blue. A one-gallon size plastic bag full of cut pieces will be enough for a group of 50 students.
- Quilt blackline master for each student.
- Record sheet for each team.
- Pencils, scissors, and glue.

DIRECTIONS TO THE STUDENTS

Opening: There are many excellent quilt stories appropriate for any age group and season. If you have time before the group lesson, read a story during your read-aloud time.

What do you know about quilts? Have you ever made one? What did you learn? Why would we make a quilt during our math time? (Students may mention symmetry, congruence, patterns, factors, colors, names of geometric shapes, area, or perimeter.)

Today we will each arrange the colored squares to create an original design on one of our quilt blocks. Choose the colors that you like in whatever arrangement you think is pleasing. You may not cut any of the pieces apart today. *(Revisit this lesson later, and let students make two triangles from their squares.)* After you have experimented with different arrangements, glue your best design down. Now, let's take a tour of the rest of the group. *(This gives other children some additional time to glue their pieces down. Students are fascinated when someone else has created a similar design. Others will benefit from the exposure to other more symmetrical, pleasing designs.)*

When you return to your spot, you are welcome to create another block using some of the new ideas you saw or another idea of your own. Glue your second block down, and cut them both out. Write your name on the backs. Complete the record sheet provided with your partner. Compare the colors you used, the shapes your quilt blocks created, look for diagonal, vertical, and horizontal symmetry, and any other ideas you have. Now join your four blocks together with masking tape on the back. What do you notice about your four-block quilt? Answer the questions on your record sheet and then compare your four-block to another team's. *(Some teams may have a six-block because they have three team members.)*

Wrap up: Have students who finish early share their observations with each other and begin to sort the quilts by common attributes.

When the buddy group has completed the quilt blocks, glue them down on large pieces of bulletin board paper for a wall display. Ask students to estimate how many buddy quilt blocks you'll have all together and what rectangle or square arrangement of blocks would work best for a quilt. Older students may want to discuss possible common factors of 24, 25, and 26 pieces. You may need an additional block to use as a filler. You can write the grades of the students participating and the teacher's names on one block and a date on a second. After you have assessed the buddy work, record an idea from each team and mount it on top of their block in the shape of talking bubbles. Comments may include ideas like "ours has diagonal symmetry," "ours doesn't look like a quilt because we didn't make a pattern," and "our quilt has an area of 36 squares." This language connection extends the learning for other students and families who may see the display.

ASSESSMENT

The record sheet provides an opportunity for students to share their understanding of quilting, symmetry, area, and perimeter. To score an advanced mark (4) on the task, students must expand the mathematical concepts beyond the obvious. This activity can be used with first- through sixth-graders based on the math vocabulary and specific skills required.

PAPER QUILTS RECORD SHEET

Names ____

You and your buddy have just completed two quilt blocks. Record your observations.

My quilt squares are______________________________________

____.

My buddy's quilt squares are_______________________________

____.

When we put our blocks together, we noticed _________________

____

____.

When we compared our blocks to other teams', we noticed __________

____

____.

Something we learned about quilts is _________________________

____.

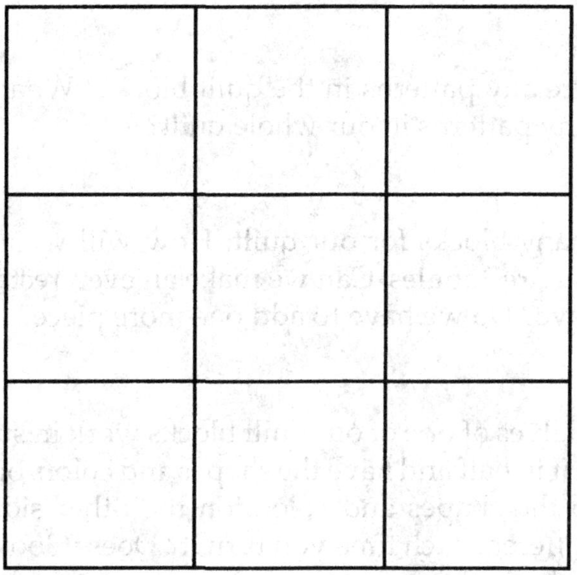

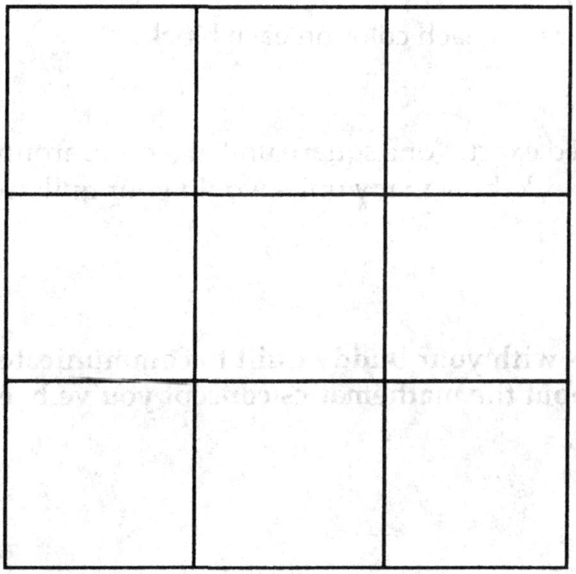

ADDRESSING MATH STANDARDS WITH QUILTING

- **Patterns**

  Do you notice any patterns in the quilt blocks? What are they? Do you notice any patterns in our whole quilt?

- **Factoring**

  We made many blocks for our quilt. How will we arrange them? Most quilts are rectangles. Can we make an even rectangle with the pieces we have? Do we have to add one more piece?

- **Symmetry**

  Do the two halves of one of our quilt blocks work in such a way that you can fold it in half and have the shapes and colors on one half flop exactly onto the shapes and colors on the other side? Does your block look different each time you turn it? Does it look the same every time? If it looks the same no matter how you turn it, we can say it has *full* rotational symmetry.

- **Area**

  How many quilt blocks are in our finished quilt?

  What is the area of each color on each block?

- **Perimeter**

  If you counted exactly one square unit at a time, around the outside of the quilt block, how many units would your quilt measure all the way around?

Display this with your buddy quilt to communicate with your audience about the mathematics concept you've been working on.

PEBBLES AND A KING

STANDARDS ADDRESSED

- Content: Number & operations and Data analysis & probability
- Process: Problem solving, communication, reasoning, and proof

MATERIALS NEEDED

- Beads, pebbles, or cubes, approximately 20 per team
- Marble or coin, one per team
- No record sheet

DIRECTIONS TO THE STUDENTS

Opening: This game originated in the Solomon Islands. Any idea where that might be? Let's find it on a map. (Look in the Pacific Ocean.) What kind of resources do you think children there have for playing games? (Rocks and sand might be an answer.)

Today each team will set up their own game on the floor. Two to five people can play this game together. Put any number of beads in a circle about the size of a dinner plate. Now add the marble. It is called the King.

The player who woke up first this morning starts. This player begins counting from one to 10 starting with the King, in a clockwise direction. Touch each bead gently as you count. Remove the 10th bead from the circle.

The second person begins counting to 10 from the very next bead. That person gets to remove the 10th bead.

The game continues until one player ends the count of 10 on the King. This player is then out of the game. If you have more than two people in your group, keep the King in the circle and continue with the other players. It is possible for the beads to be all gone and with just the King left. In that case, both players are winners.

Wrap up: Have all the students clean up their game and share their strategies for winning. Is it skill or luck? Does it matter how many beads you start with? Does it matter how many people you play with?

Comment: Some weeks you may be inundated with pencil-and-paper work. This game is a great one to play with buddies and then send home as a family connection. Send home the directions with a sandwich bag full of game manipulatives. The students love to challenge friends and family to a game they know well. Because the game is both chance and skill, even the youngest child can win.

ASSESSMENT

This activity has no record sheet. Therefore, teacher observation is critical. Younger students should count with a one-to-one correspondence. Older students may count by twos or groups of fives. Frequently, students will anticipate their next turn and cleverly skip a bead in counting if no one is looking! This peaks everyone's participation. During the wrap-up discussion, students may share that they noticed theories like the person who started won more often. Students may have an assumption about the odd and even number of beads in relationship to the winner. Encourage them to defend their hypothesis with experiences they had during their games.

PROBABILITY EXPERIMENT

STANDARDS ADDRESSED

- Content: Number & operations and Data analysis & probability
- Process: Problem solving, communication, reasoning, and proof

MATERIALS NEEDED

- Six-sided cube pattern for each team
- Record sheet for each team
- Pencils, crayons, scissors, and tape

DIRECTIONS TO THE STUDENTS

Opening: This is the cube I made. Notice I wrote my favorite color twice on the cube. If I roll it 20 times, which color do you think I will roll most often? Why? What else do you know about chance or probability?

Today each team will create a cube using your favorite numbers, letters, pictures, or colors. You can "weigh" the chances of one of the choices winning, by using it more than once. Cut the cube pattern out along the outside black lines and fold on the dotted lines. Tape the cube together and you're ready to go. Predict what you think will happen and why.

Turn your paper over and write your choices in the columns on the graph.

With your buddy's help, record the results of the first 10 rolls. Record the results by coloring the units on the graph with a crayon. Don't forget to stop at 10.

After 10 rolls, reevaluate your prediction. Do you want to change your original prediction? Why or why not?

Continue rolling your cube another 10 times and record the results with another color crayon. Answer the questions on your record sheet.

Wrap up: Have students who finish early share their strategies for record keeping and graphing with each other. Did any team experiment turn our differently than they predicted? Why or Why not? What is probability? Where else in their day-to-day life does probability come in to play?

ASSESSMENT

The record sheet provides an opportunity for students to share their understanding of probability and data analysis. To score an advanced mark (4) on the task, students must synthesize these mathematical concepts. This activity can be adapted for younger grades by rolling only 10 times and having the older buddies record the numeric analysis of the experiment. Encourage students to record the results in mathematically interesting comparison statements like "we rolled two more A's than B's," "there were twice as many blue as yellow," and "we had half as many fours as sixes."

PROBABILITY WITH MATH BUDDIES

Names____

Today each of you will set up a probability experiment with a six-sided cube. You can draw a color, number, or picture for each of the squares on your cube pattern. You can "weigh" the chances of one of the choices winning, by recording it twice. Cut the cube out along the dark black lines and fold on the dotted lines. Tape the cube together and you're ready to go! Before you begin, predict what you think will happen and why.

I predict ____

because ____

____

Record your choices in the columns provided.

15						
14						
13						
12						
11						
10						
9						
8						
7						
6						
5						
4						
3						
2						
1						
Choices						

Color in the results of the *first 10 rolls* on the graph.
Was your prediction accurate? Why or why not?

Roll 10 more times. What happened after all 20 rolls and why?

If you rolled another 20 times, what do you think would happen?

What is probability?

PROBABILITY EXPERIMENT

Cut out the shape.

Which geometric solid can you make by folding along the dotted lines?

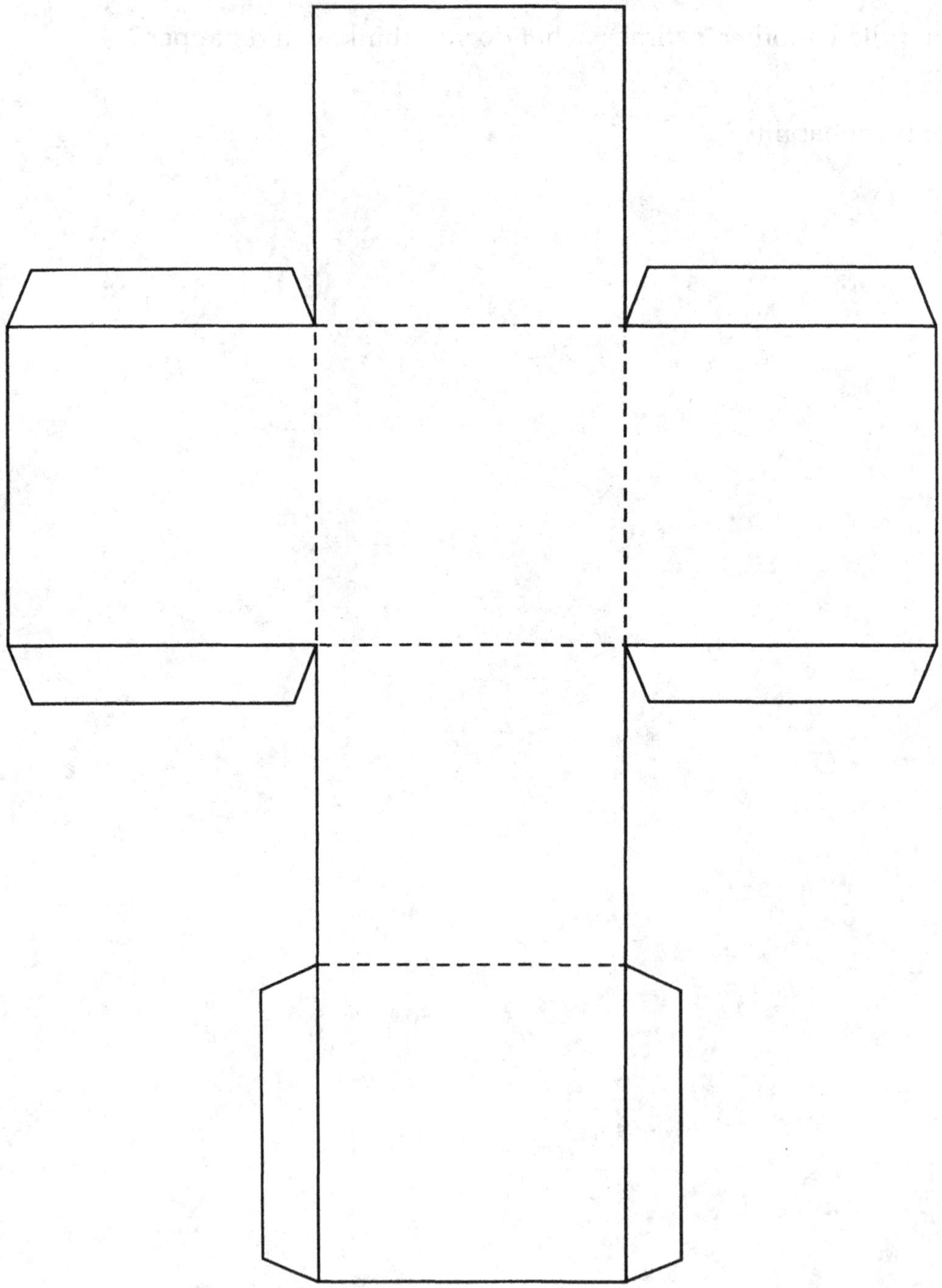

SNOWFLAKE SYMMETRY, AN AREA LESSON

STANDARDS ADDRESSED

- Content: Number & operations, Geometry, and Measurement
- Process: Problem solving, connections, and representation

MATERIALS NEEDED

- 9-inch square of construction paper in two different colors; one color will represent each class. For instance, older buddies will use red squares and the younger buddies will use black squares.
- Pattern blocks shape, one page of each, run on white paper per team.
- Record sheet for each student.
- Pencils, scissors, and glue.

DIRECTIONS TO THE STUDENTS

Opening: Have you ever looked closely at a snowflake? What did you notice? *(Students may answer that they are all different. They have symmetry. They are like crystals.)*

Today we will use four different geometric shapes to create our very own snowflake. Who can name this shape? *(Hold up a triangle.)* Tell your buddy the name of this shape. Now tell your buddy the name of this shape. *(Hold up a rhombus.)* Let's check with the group. What did you think this was? *(Students answer rhombus or parallelogram.)*

If the triangle had an area of one, what would the area of the rhombus shape be? (Students answer two. Teacher demonstrates that two triangles equal the area of one rhombus.)

Look at the next shape. *(Hold up a trapezoid.)* Whisper the name of this shape to your buddy. What did you think it is? Did everyone know this is a trapezoid? What would the area of this trapezoid be? How many of these triangles would I need to cover the top of this trapezoid? *(Students should answer three. They may have added one triangle and one rhombus, 1 + 2 = 3, or three triangles together, 1 + 1 + 1 = 3.)* How did you know that?

Let's look at the last shape. *(Hold up a hexagon.)* Share your idea with your buddy. What is the name of this shape? *(Students guess lots of possibilities like octagon, pentagon, etc.)* Hexagons have six sides. Count them with me to be sure. Yes, this one has six equal sides.

What is the area of my hexagon shape? Discuss it with your buddy and share your thinking, too. I heard many of you say six. Who will share how they knew the area was six? Two trapezoids equal one hexagon, 3 + 3 = 6. Three rhombi equal a hexagon, 2 + 2 + 2 = 6. Six triangles equal one hexagon, 1 + 1 + 1 + 1 + 1 + 1 = 6. Does anyone have any other solutions?

Now we're ready to work. Each team of buddies will get a set of white triangles, rhombi, trapezoids and hexagon shapes. Cut out several of each shape and begin designing a snowflake pattern. Remember that snowflakes are symmetrical. They are the same on two sides. Ask your buddy to check your snowflake for symmetry. When you have created a design you like, glue it down.

Use the record sheet provided to find the total area of your snowflake. Count the triangles, rhombi, trapezoids, and hexagons you used in your design. Record the area of each shape. Have your buddy help you figure the combined area. Can you think of some other features of your snowflake that makes it unique? Write your ideas down.

Wrap up: Have students who finish early share their observations with each other and sort the snowflakes by common attributes.

When the buddy group has completed the snowflake, create a quilt pattern using alternating color blocks for a wall display. Ask students to estimate how many buddy quilt blocks you'll have all together and what rectangle or square arrangement of blocks would work best for a quilt. Older students may want to discuss possible common factors of 48, 50, and 52 pieces. You may need an additional block to use as a filler. You can write the names of the students and teachers on one block and the date on a second. After you have assembled the buddy work, record a comment from each team on a talking bubble and mount it on top of their snowflake. Comments may include ideas like "ours has diagonal symmetry" and "our snowflake has an area of 36 squares." This language connection extends the learning for other students and families that read the display.

ASSESSMENT

The record sheet provides an opportunity for students to share their understanding of symmetry, area, and geometry. To score an advanced mark (4) on the task, students must synthesize the mathematical concepts presented. This activity can be used with first- through sixth-graders based on the math vocabulary and support for the computation skills required.

SNOWFLAKE SYMMETRY

Name ____

Today we made snowflakes from triangles, rhombi, trapezoids, and hexagons. Here's how you can find mine:

I used _____ triangles with an area of one unit. _____

I used _____ rhombi with an area of ______units. _____

I used _____ trapezoids with an area of _____units. _____

I used _____ hexagons with an area of _____units. _____

The total area of my snowflake design was __________

Other things I noticed about my snowflake are ____________________

____

____.

TRIANGLE

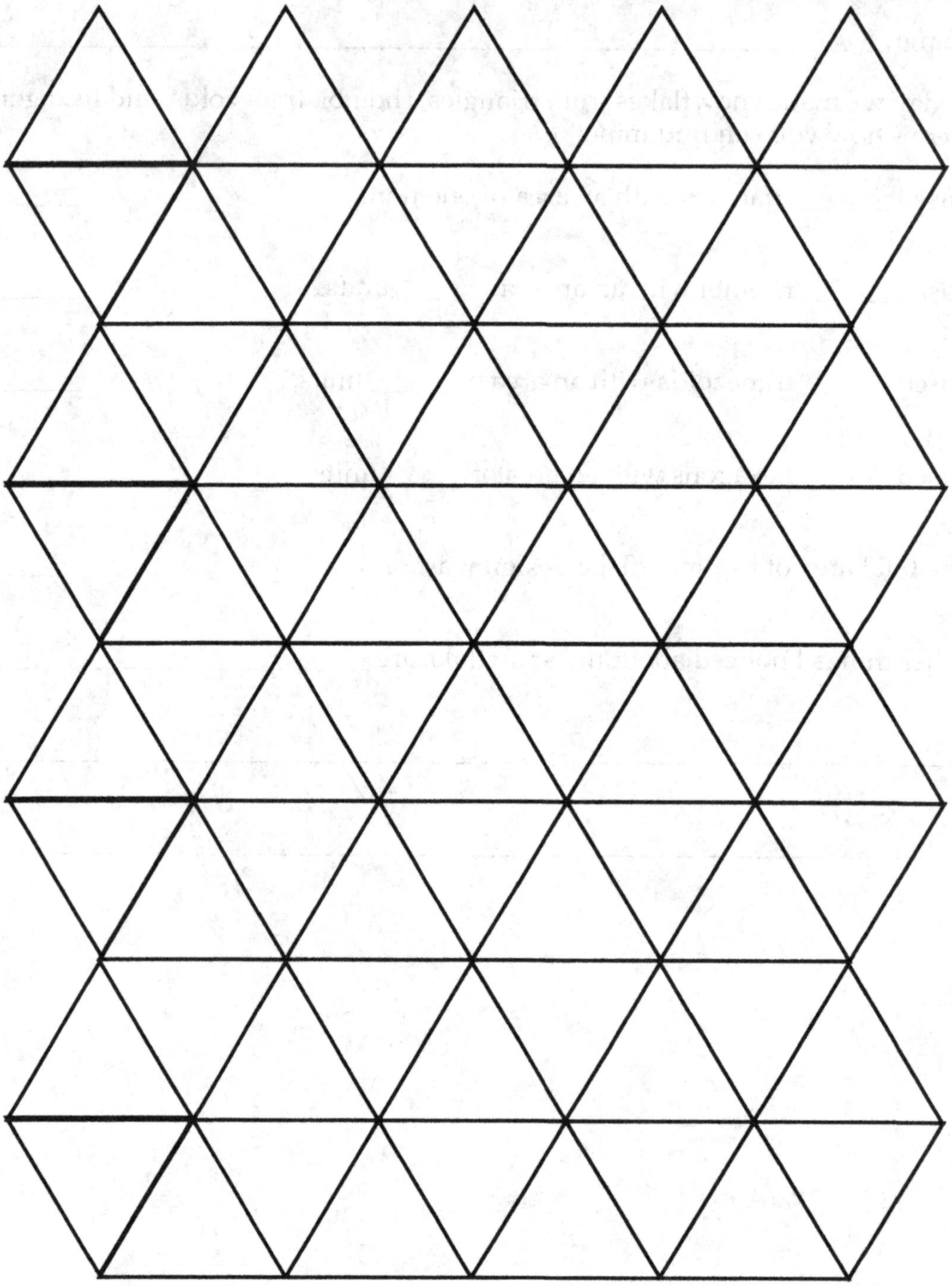

RHOMBUS

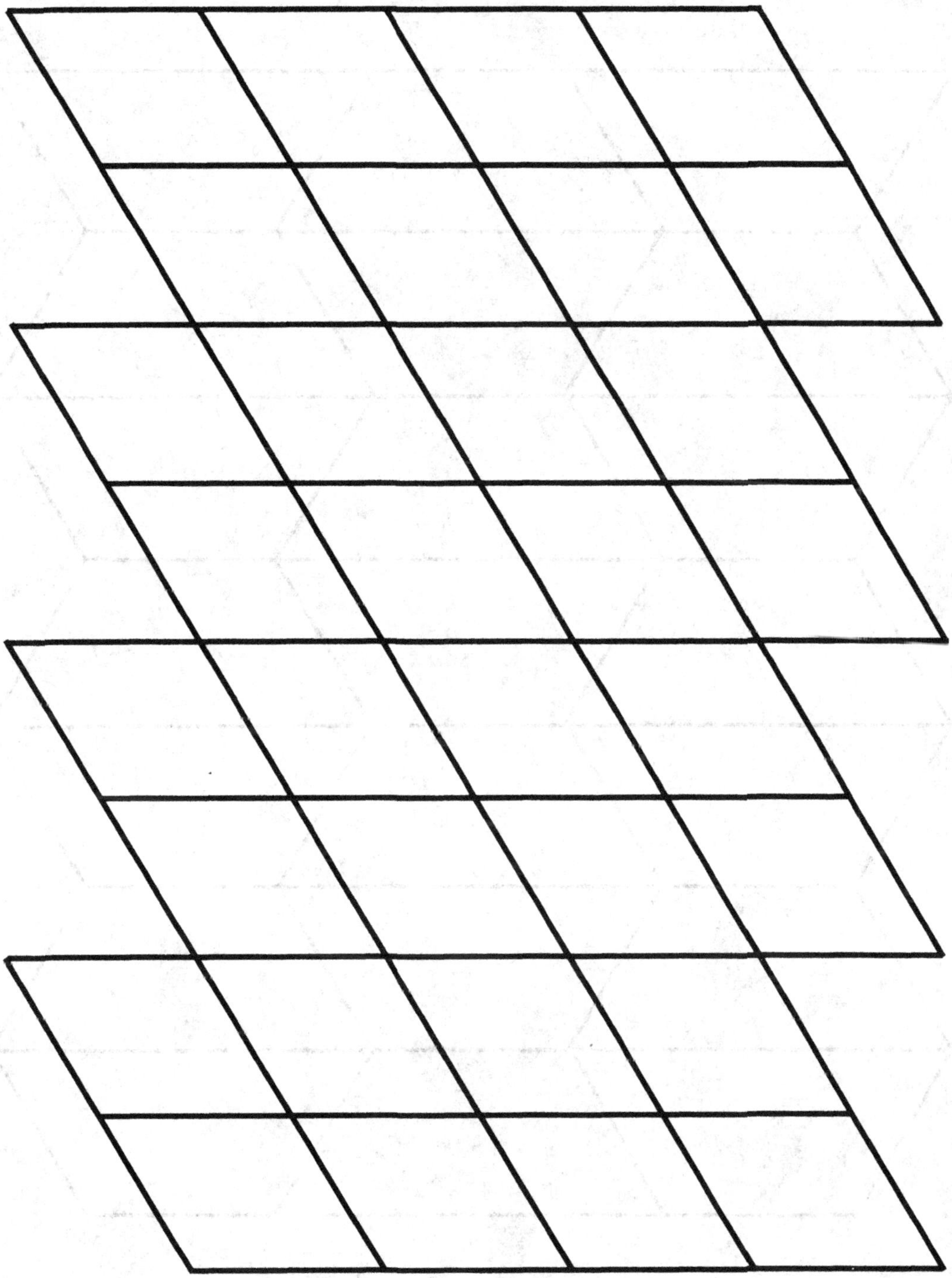

HEXAGON

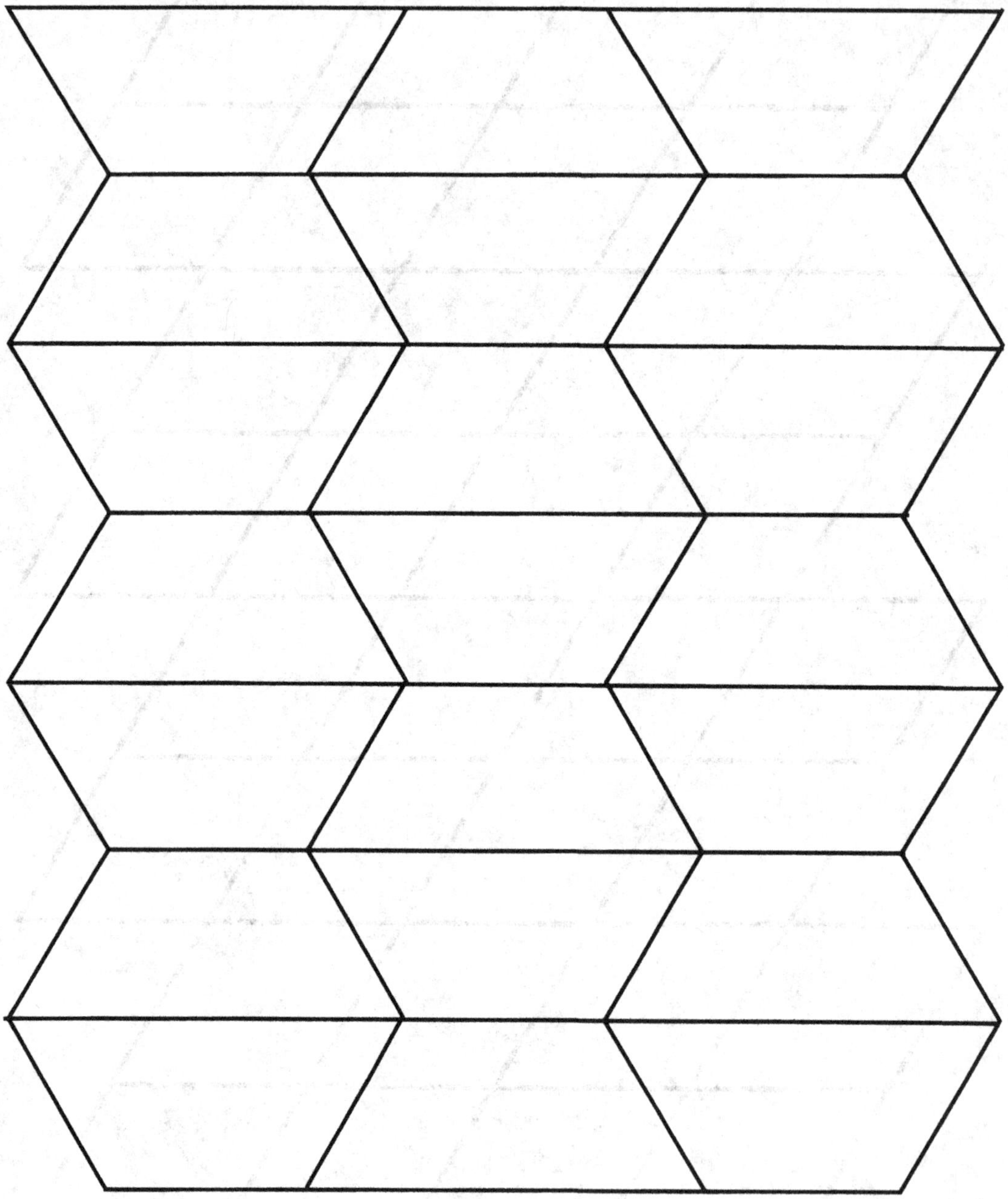

TRAPEZOID

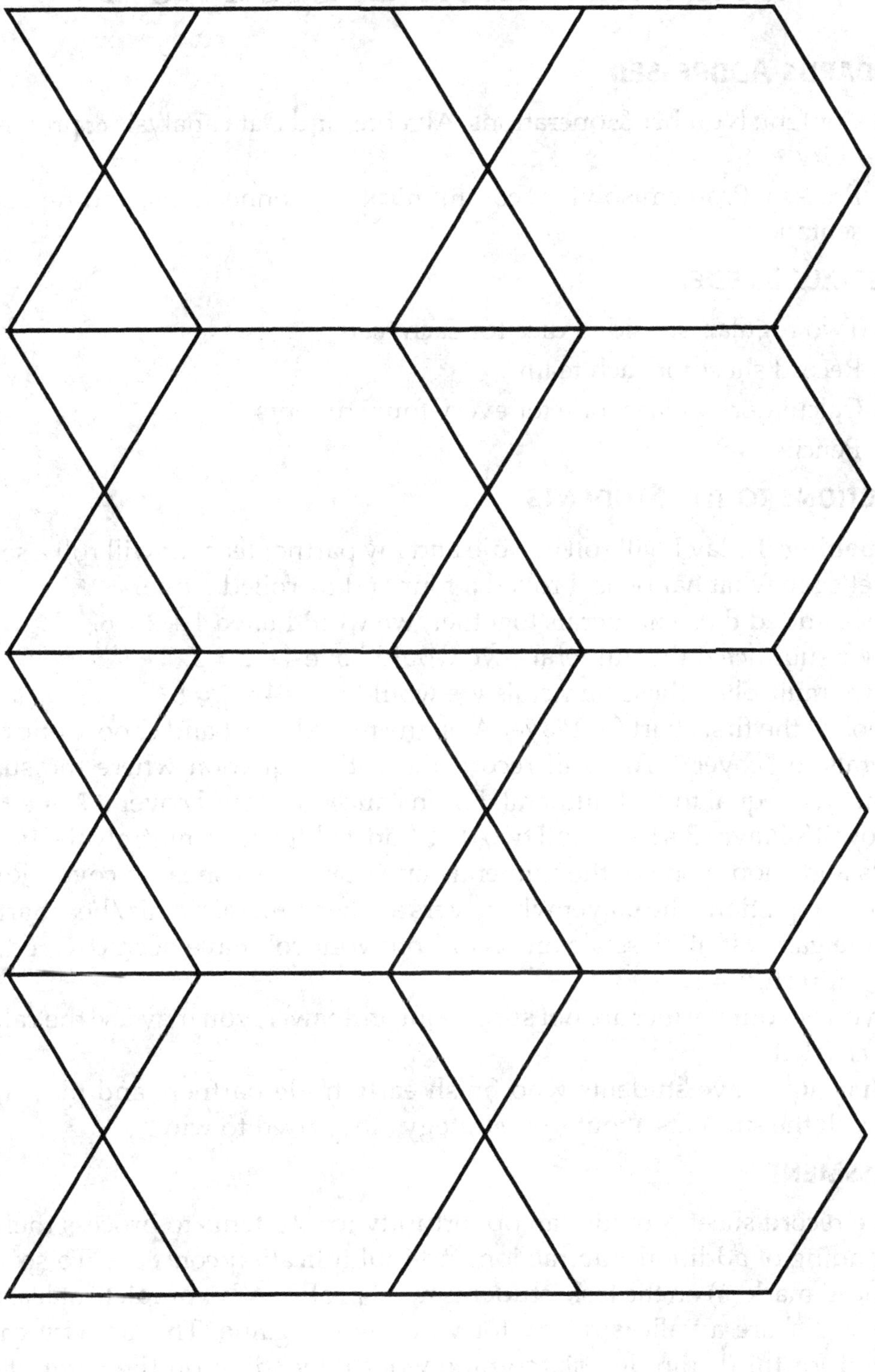

STRATEGY WITH BASIC FACTS

STANDARDS ADDRESSED

- Content: Number & operations, Algebra, and Data analysis & probability
- Process: Problem solving, communication, connections, and representation

MATERIALS NEEDED

- Two regular, six-sided dice for each team
- Record sheet for each team
- Calculators, at least one for every four students
- Pencils

DIRECTIONS TO THE STUDENTS

Opening: Today I will roll one die and my partner teacher will roll a second die. Let's see what happens. I rolled a four and he rolled a two.

If we added those numerals together, we would have 4 + 2 = 6.

If we subtracted the numerals, we would have 4 – 2 = 2.

If we multiplied these numerals we would have 4 x 2 = 8.

Look at the first chart for Player A on the record sheet and choose one of the numerals to "cover." You will record the entire equation where the sum or product was equal to that numeral. For instance, we could cover a 2 or a 6.

Now it's Player B's turn. Roll two die. Add, subtract, or multiply the two numerals and choose one of the numerals on your record sheet to cover. Record the entire equation. The player who covers all the numerals in his/her chart first wins the game. If all possible answers from your roll have been covered, you lose your turn.

If you or your partner are not sure about an answer, you may use the calculator to check it.

Wrap up: Have students who finish early trade partners and play again. Visit with the students about the "strategy" they used to win.

ASSESSMENT

The record sheet provides an opportunity for students to process their understanding of addition, subtraction and multiplication concepts. To score an advanced mark (4) on the task, students must proficiently complete at least one game and share a valid strategy for winning the game. This activity can be adapted for third- through sixth-grade work depending on the computation standards for the grade levels involved. Second graders can play with addition and subtraction concepts. Fourth graders can include division concepts when they are ready.

STRATEGY WITH BASIC FACTS RECORD SHEET

Names ______________________________

Player	A		Player	B
0	7		0	7
1	8		1	8
2	9		2	9
3	10		3	10
4	11		4	11
5	12		5	12
6	0		6	0

What strategies did you use to win? ______________________________

____

____

TAPE MEASURES

STANDARDS ADDRESSED

- Content: Number & operations and Measurement
- Process: Problem solving, communication, connection, and representation

MATERIALS NEEDED

- Tape measure blackline master for each student
- Record sheet for each team
- Pencils, scissors, and glue

DIRECTIONS TO THE STUDENTS

Opening: Read *Inch by Inch* by Leo Lioni during your read-aloud time.

What can we use to measure things? Students may answer cubes, links, tiles, scales, weights, tape measures, rulers, and yard and meter sticks. You may want to mention that tape measures are excellent tools because they are flexible and can be used for the circumference of our heads, waists, ankles, and other curved surfaces.

Today we will each make a tape measure of our own. Look at the record sheet with the tape measure pattern. The tape is separated in four segments and needs to be cut out on the black lines and put together in numerical order. Be careful not to cut the adjoining flaps. We need them to overlap for the glue.

Younger buddies will use the inch side of the tape and the older buddies will use the centimeter side. Your team will choose 10 things around the room to measure. Before you measure, be sure that both of you have made an estimate. The younger buddy will use her/his tape to measure in inches and record the results. The older buddy will use the centimeter markings to measure and record the actual measurement of the same thing.

When you have completed the activity, write at least two statements about what you learned.

Wrap up: Have students who finish early share their observations with each other and measure and record other things in the room.

ASSESSMENT

The record sheet provides an opportunity for students to communicate their understanding of number, estimation skills, and the relationship between inches and centimeters. To score an advanced mark (4) on the task, students must expand the concept of measurement beyond the grade level expectations. This activity can be adapted for first- through sixth-grade work depending on the benchmarks for each grade level. Older buddies benefit from the exposure to both inches and centimeters and are able to compare these standard units.

BUDDY WORK WITH TAPE MEASURES

Names____

Today we will each make a tape measure. We will use it to measure 10 items. The younger buddy will record how many inches he/she estimates it will measure. Then, the older buddy will estimate in centimeters. Measure the items and then record the actual amount in both inches and centimeters.

Name of Item	*Estimated Inches*	*Actual Inches*	*Estimated Centimeters*	*Actual Centimeters*

We learned ____

____

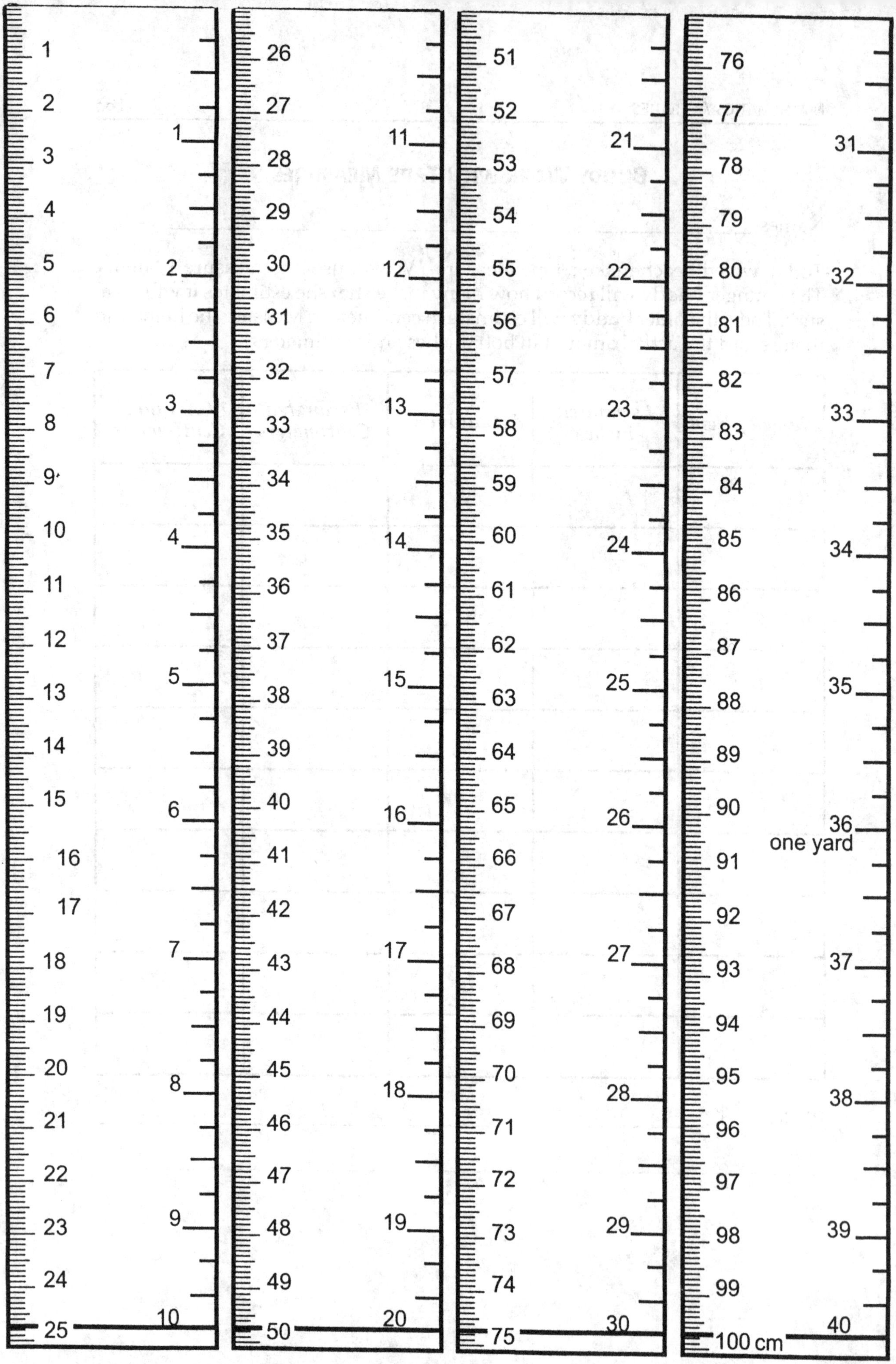
one yard
100 cm

Name ______________________________ is certified to be a

COOL BUDDY

Date ____________________ Signed ____________________

9781930556157